VOICES OF
TWELVE HEBREW PROPHETS

Voices of
Twelve Hebrew Prophets

COMMONLY CALLED
THE MINOR PROPHETS

G. CAMPBELL MORGAN, D.D.

BAKER BOOK HOUSE
Grand Rapids, Michigan

Reprinted 1975 by
Baker Book House
ISBN: 0-8010-5977-1

First printing, September 1975
Second printing, April 1977
Third printing, October 1979
Fourth printing, March 1982

PHOTOLITHOPRINTED BY CUSHING - MALLOY, INC.
ANN ARBOR, MICHIGAN, UNITED STATES OF AMERICA

CONTENTS

12   36

INTRODUCTORY

The Prophetic Office

SCRIPTURE LESSON: ACTS 3.

"Yet the Lord testified unto Israel, and unto Judah, by the hand of every prophet, and of every seer, saying, Turn ye from your evil ways, and keep My commandments and My statutes; according to all the law which I commanded your fathers, and which I sent to you by the hand of My servants the prophets."
—2 KINGS 17:13.

THE New Testament uniformly assumes that the prophets spake from God. In this passage from the Second Book of the Kings we have the outstanding statement revealing the place of the prophet, the authority of the prophet, and the message of the prophet.

It is the habit of many today to undervalue the old Hebrew prophets, and to declare that with the New Testament in our hands, we do not need their messages. A writer in the recent issue of the *Poetry Review*, under the heading, "Whither Poetry?" said:

"Prophets are too many and too confusing in the blur of their own visions to be accepted by a scientific and time-conscious age."

Necessarily, her reference may have been to modern prophets. If so, I should find myself in agreement with what she says. If, however, the reference is to the Hebrew prophets, I should join issue with the statement. Her phrase "time-conscious" is in itself a revealing one, and shows largely what is the matter with the age. It is time-conscious. It is forgetting the measurements of the ages. The definition, however, does not apply to the Hebrew prophets. Whereas their messages were for the age in which they were delivered, they all breathed the spirit of eternal things.

In the series of sermons now beginning we shall attempt to show how the messages delivered by these men in the long ago have a direct bearing upon life at all times, and so necessarily upon our own times.

The period of the history of Israel which was specifically and specially that of the prophet lasted for about five hundred years, from the beginning of the ninth to the beginning of the fourth centuries B.C. After that there was no prophetic voice until that of John the Baptist. The prophetic gift, of course, had occurred occasionally long before the period referred to. Peter in the message of the Lesson said, "All the prophets from Samuel," thus going back far from the period to which we are now referring. During this period, however, these prophets were in the Divine economy, the authoritative voices, dictating terms to kings, upbraiding the failing people, and indicating what their true line of policy and of activity should be. These Hebrew prophets ever kept before the people the supreme fact that the Hebrew nation was a Theocracy, and that it was a nation created to live among the other nations, a revelation of what it means to have God as actual King. The nation was purely and simply a Theocracy under Moses, and through the period of the Judges. Then there came the hour of the fall of the nation from

Theocracy to monarchy. The account of that is found in the declaration made by God, to Samuel, concerning the clamor of the people for a king:

"They have not rejected thee; but they have rejected Me, that I should not be King over them."

Following a principle of the Divine government, God gave them what they asked, and Saul reigned for forty years, David for forty years, and Solomon for forty years. Then followed the catastrophe, and the Kingdom was rent in twain, Israel and Judah. We have the appalling story of kings succeeding each other often by the murder of their predecessor. During this whole period God was still King, and when these earthly kings became utterly corrupted, the prophetic office was born, and from that moment until it ceased after Malachi, it was through the prophets, not the king, nor the priests, that God spoke to the people.

Thus the whole of that period is covered by the words with which we began:

"The Lord testified unto Israel, and unto Judah, by the hand of every prophet, and of every seer, saying, Turn ye from your evil ways, and keep My commandments and My statutes; according to all the law which I commanded your fathers, and which I sent to you by the hand of My servants the prophets."

As we turn, therefore, to a consideration of the prophetic messages there are three elements discoverable. First, there is that of the application of their message to their own age, which need not detain us. The age is past. The actors have gone. Conditions have changed, but it was a Divine message applicable in every case to the age in which it was uttered.

The second element is that out of the midst of existing conditions these prophets were ever looking forward, and so we have what may be described as the predictive element. This is clearly found throughout.

The third element is that of the abiding application of principles to all times. That for us is the supreme value of these writings. It may be said that the times have changed, and that is at once admitted. But the principles have not changed.

Their message to their own age was always, first, that of the sovereignty of God. These messengers did not argue for that very much, but declared its application. Their protests were all against that which was contrary to the Divine authority. Their intention was ever that of the glory of the Name of God. Their hope was always centered in Him.

As to their predictions, throughout we find them foretelling the failure of the chosen people. They also foretold the coming of Messiah, and the realization under Him of the purposes of God on the earth. The first element has been fulfilled. The chosen people have failed, and they have been excommunicated from the economy of God. The second has been fulfilled in the fact that Messiah has come, and the realization under His rule, of the fulfilment of the purpose of God, is going forward; and His Kingdom will yet be established over the whole earth. The third element, that of the underlying principles, will create the burden of our meditations on these messages of the Hebrew prophets to our own time.

In the Old Testament we have a body of prophetic writings consisting of the utterances of sixteen prophets. They have been commonly divided into Major and Minor. The only sense in which twelve of them are called Minor is that they are less in bulk. Certainly they are not less in importance. In the Hebrew Bible we have twelve of these known as The Book of the Twelve.

In this meditation I want us in the briefest way to survey the whole of these writings. Necessarily I am not attempting anything in the nature of full exposition, but I propose to pass rapidly over these sixteen prophetic utterances that we may gain a general sense of them. In subsequent meditations we shall confine ourselves to the Twelve. In surveying them I am not taking them in the order in which we find them in our Bibles, but in historic sequence.

Isaiah was supremely the prophet of the Theocracy. He declared the judgment that must fall upon the nation which failed to fulfil its mission in the world. He nevertheless clearly foresaw the ultimate victory of God through an appointed Servant, Who through travail should bring in the triumph.

Jeremiah was Jehovah's spokesman in the days of darkness and disaster. Through personal suffering he delivered his messages of punishment and of promise in days when neither the one nor the other was received by the people. By all our ordinary statistics no result followed his ministry, but he heroically carried it out. In the little sheaf of poems which we call the Lamentations we find him voicing the suffering of the nation as one who had intimate relationship with God, and felt it most acutely.

Ezekiel, in the dark days of exile, bore testimony supremely to the glory of God. This was manifested in his reprobation of the nation which had failed, and his foretelling of the ultimate restoration of all things to allegiance to the Throne.

Daniel was the prophet of hope in a time of dense darkness. Out of the midst of historic night he spoke in the language of prophetic light. In every one of these four, commonly called Major, we find the same fundamental truths, the sovereignty of God, and the failure and punishment of His people. But none of them ended on that note. Every one saw through to a glory and a victory which was yet to come.

Joel saw the nation under the government of God, and insistently proclaimed the day of Jehovah as to its government and as to its grace.

The book of Jonah is a prophetic story indicating the inclusiveness of the Divine government for Nineveh as well as Israel; and rebuking the exclusiveness of the Hebrew nation as manifested in the prophet himself.

Amos was supremely conscious of the people as a nation, and uttered the message of national accountability to the government of God in its application to surrounding nations, and preëminently to Israel and Judah.

Hosea, through his own broken heart, viewed the

nation in its spiritual relation to God, and showed that its sin was that of spiritual infidelity and adultery.

Obadiah was concerned with the attitude of Edom towards Israel, and denounced the same in the name of the reigning God.

Micah's vision was largely that of the governing center of authority, and from that standpoint he condemned the false rulers and proclaimed the appointment of the true.

Nahum was the complement of Jonah one hundred years later. He declared the overthrow of Nineveh which had been spared, under the preaching of Jonah, on account of its repentance. His message was delivered to the nation as it was returning from captivity, and it consisted of a message of warning and of encouragement.

Zephaniah spoke from the standpoint of an intimate knowledge of God. He declared His severity and His goodness, showing that these things are not in opposition, but in apposition.

Habakkuk delivered a message as he gave an account of his own experience as a man of faith, perplexed by the circumstances of the hour, who found a great solution which he declared to the nation.

Haggai understood that relationship to God was the true secret of national strength, and urged the rebuilding of the temple.

Zechariah coöperated with Haggai, and became the great prophet in Hebrew history concerning the final things.

Malachi condemned the corruption of formal accuracy, the maintenance of form devoid of power, and ended his message by predictions concerning the coming One.

Thus throughout all these prophetic utterances we find first a recognition of the Throne of God, a proclamation of His sovereignty, also always the denunciation of infidelity to that Throne as the sin of all sins, with the declaration that such infidelity must bring its nemesis of judgment and suffering. In every case, however, these Hebrew prophets saw through the murk and the mist the glory that is yet to come. Not one of them was a pessimist. Each was an optimist. Nevertheless, not one of them was an optimist blind to the conditions in the midst of which he was living. There is no question that these Hebrew prophets have a voice for our own times.

As we give attention to these voices of the Twelve we remember that the background all the way through is that of the failure of a privileged people. It is unquestionably a terrible story, and following through as a story we find its culmination in the crucifixion of the Son of God. To such conditions these men were delivering messages, and in them revealing the vital and abiding principles of life.

These principles are still supreme. Man has not changed, that is, humanity has not changed. All that the prophets said needs saying today, and that with no uncertain sound. Kings and statesmen and politicians, and humanity generally, need to be called back to God, and back to His Throne in a great repentance, that is, a change of mind. The New Testament distinctly declares: "To Him bear all the prophets witness." That is true, but for the moment I venture to take that great statement and put it in another form. He is the Fulfilment of everything to which the prophets bare their witness. They spoke of the sovereignty of God, but it was finally and fully declared through Christ. They declared that men, forgetful of that sovereignty, and breaking the laws of God, were doomed to punishment. That Christ made clear as the sunlight. They looked on to a day of ultimate victory and triumph, and in all His messages to men that' fact is most clearly revealed.

I

THE VOICE OF JOEL

The Day of the Lord

SCRIPTURE LESSON: JOEL 1:14, 15; 2:1, 2, 11b-14, 28-32; 3:14.
"The day of the Lord is at hand."—JOEL 1:15.

I T is not possible to be dogmatic as to the date of
the prophecy of Joel. The study of the book itself makes it evident that he was one of the earliest or one of the latest of the prophets. The matter
is not of any particular importance. Personally, I believe he was one of the earliest, and therefore we take
him first in our series.

The burden of his message is revealed in the phrase
"the day of Jehovah," which occurs five times in the
course of the book, and that in connection with a threefold outlook.

The first phase of this was that of his vision of
things that were near, of the circumstances in the midst
of which he and those to whom he spoke were then
living. An actual plague of locusts had swept over the
land, and the first part of his message was that of
an interpretation of the desolation resulting from that
plague.

The second phase was born of his consciousness of a
serious judgment that was threatening the people, that,
namely, of the coming of an invading army, which he

described, using the figure of the locust plague for purposes of illustration. This was followed by a distinct
interpolation on his part, in which he foretold the day
of the poured-out Spirit.

Then the third phase was his foretelling of a distant
Day of the Lord which would be one of final judgment,
leading to the complete establishment of the Divine
sovereignty.

In every message he saw the activity of Jehovah.
Looking around at the results of the locust plague,
looking ahead and seeing the imminent invasion, and
at last looking to the things of the far distances, he
recognized in all the Day of the Lord.

It may be said that the whole prophecy is the result
of a vision in perspective of the highway of Jehovah
through the centuries. The prophet saw that the Day
of the Lord was ever present, and that fact constituted
the burden of his prophesying. As we listen to his
voice we discover the principles of the Divine government, and we are given in outline a revelation of the
plan of God in the ages. Throughout he is showing
the application of the principles of the reign of Jehovah. These principles are seen to consist of government and grace.

As to government, throughout we are made conscious of the enthroned Jehovah. Whatever were the
signs of the times, whatever the defection of the people, whatever the perils threatening them, Jehovah is
still enthroned, and is seen presiding in patience over
all the processes through which His people pass; press-
ing into His service all forces, the forces of Nature, the

locusts; human forces, a coming army; and finally, asserting Himself in absolutely and unqualified victory. Wherever Joel looked he was conscious of the Day of the Lord. The final Day as he saw it is still postponed, but it is absolutely certain. Joel saw very far afield as is proven by the fact that the ultimate things he predicted have not yet taken place. He saw the near things, the sin of his people, and the locust plague; the imminent things, the coming of judgment, and the restoration following it; the far things, the Day of the Spirit, and the culminating activities following that Day.

As to grace, throughout the teaching of the prophet, the fact that grace is the inspiration of government is ever revealed. It is seen acting as the restraint upon judgment, so that when the locust plague was under consideration, it led to an appeal to the people to repent. Moreover when declaring the judgment that was imminent, he made appeal on behalf of God to the people to return to Him, rending their heart rather than their garments. When he is dealing with the ultimate triumph through processes of judgment, that triumph is described not as that of a conqueror who rejoices that he has crushed, but that of a Conqueror Who gives peace and beauty. Thus the issue of government is also grace, beneficent, glorious, and beautiful.

These principles of government and grace are illustrated first in the case of the locust plague. Of such a plague men would be inclined to say, It is a sore misfortune. It could not be foreseen, neither could it be prevented. It had swept over the country and caused

such devastation that, as the prophet declared, there
was no wine for the drunkards, no offerings for the
Temple, and the people throughout the land were lacking bread. The prophet's message to the people was
that this unforeseen and unpreventable catastrophe was
none other than the act of God. The age was forgetting God, and Joel stood amid the devastation and declared that the events of which men would speak as
happenings in the course of Nature were, as a matter
of fact, the immediate actions of God. The locust
plague was therefore the Day of the Lord. He called
upon the old men and the drunkards, the possessors of
the land, and all the people to a recognition of this fact.

In his graphic description, as we have said, using the
figure of the locust plague, of the imminent invasion of
an army, he declared:

"The Lord uttereth His voice before His army."
and thus called upon them to recognize the invading
foe as acting under the authority of God.

When looking on he described the final things, his
message was clearly a prophecy of the coming forth of
God in judgment, leading on to the realization of Divine purpose, Thus whether Joel looked at the rear, the
imminent, or the distant, he insisted upon the presence
and the activity of God. Throughout all these movements he illustrated with equal clarity the fact of the
Divine grace. The call to repentance in the first application in the case of the locust plague presupposes the
patient grace of the Divine heart. In his dealing with
the imminent invasion, a declaraton is made:

"Yet even now, saith the Lord, turn ye unto Me

with all your heart, and with fasting, and with weeping, and with mourning; and rend your heart, and not your garments, and turn unto the Lord your God; for He is gracious and full of compassion, slow to anger, and plenteous in mercy, and repenteth Him of the evil."

Thus the underlying purpose of government is seen to be grace, as in this message of God He declared that He will change His mind concerning judgment when men change their mind, and in repentance turn back to Him. He is slow to anger, and halts the march of His wrath in order that men may repent.

When we come to the final movement the grace is equally manifest.

"I will show wonders in the heavens and in the earth, blood, and fire, and pillars of smoke."

That is indeed a description of the great ultimate and terrible Day of the Lord; but even then His grace will wait:

"For in mount Zion and in Jerusalem there shall be those that escape, as the Lord hath said, and among the remnant those whom the Lord doth call."

Again attending to the voice of Joel we have a revelation of a Divine plan. Looking onward he saw beyond the circumstances in the midst of which he uttered his messages, and beyond those which should immediately follow, and before the dawning of the ultimate Day of judgment, he saw a period undated and unmeasured, and yet full of gracious and wonderful blessing. From the judgment in the midst of which men were living, and from the judgment imminent a way of deliv-

erance was promised. Then he introduces his reference
to the period we have referred to, with the words:

"It shall come to pass afterward, that I will pour
out My Spirit."

Of course we are familiar with the meaning of that remarkable utterance because we have our New Testament in our hands, and find therein the declaration of
the apostle on the day of Pentecost:

"This is that which hath been spoken by the
prophet Joel."

Joel saw in outline that which he could not perfectly
describe, and yet that which he did so accurately describe. His word "afterward" shows that he could not
definitely place it in the course of history. We know
that it lay at least five centuries away from the time in
which he uttered his prophecy. This foretelling was
most remarkable as that of a Hebrew prophet, because
it predicted the outpouring of the Spirit upon all flesh.
He saw, moreover, that that outpouring would produce
results irrespective of caste, not merely upon the
favored such as kings, princes, priests, and rulers, but
also upon the bondslaves.

Then beyond that age of the Spirit he saw other
activities of the Divine government. He indicated the
end of the period of the Spirit, and the beginning of
the final movement by the words:

"I will show wonders in the heavens and in the
earth, blood, and fire, and pillars of smoke. The sun
shall be turned into darkness, and the moon into
blood, before the great and terrible day of the Lord
come."

These are not the signs of the age of the Spirit, but signs which indicate its close, and the ushering in of a final Day of judgment. Thus looking at the near, the imminent and the distant, there was revealed the fact that the ideals and purposes of God were in process, moving to final and full accomplishment.

As we follow the reasoning of Joel there are certain things which constitute its message to our own day. The first is a recognition of the tremendous fact that the Day of the Lord is always present, and is always coming. There are those who deny that there ever will be a Day of the Lord in which He will come in judgment. On the other hand there are those who are ever looking forward to the future Day of the Lord, forgetting that this is also the Day of the Lord. God is active in the hour in which we live. There is a sense in which it may be said that this is man's day. We live in an age of remarkable progress. Inventions are multiplied hourly. Human culture has reached a level never before attained, and all these things are calculated to make man think that he is independent of God. There is a widespread tendency to the deification of human reason and ability. The results are disastrous to all that is highest and best in human life. The voice of the prophet declares, however, that even though apparently it is the day of man, it is also the Day of the Lord. The activities in the midst of which we find ourselves are all carried on in the atmosphere of the Divine presence and over-ruling. It was Isaiah who asked the question:

"Who among us shall dwell with the devouring

fire? Who among us shall dwell with everlasting burnings?"

All human events are going forward in the midst of that fire and of those burnings. In answer to Isaiah's question as to who can dwell in it, he replied:

"He that walketh righteously, and speaketh uprightly."

Whatever human activities may be they cannot escape this fact of the Divine presence and activity; and in the long issue only those things are permanent which are the things of righteousness. Every age will repeat this process until the final one when, through the last activities, God will realize the purposes upon which His heart is set. As we have said more than once, through all the movements there are evidences of His grace.

For us it is of the utmost importance that we should recognize where we are in this plan of the ages. We live in the age of the outpoured Spirit, and the message we are called upon to deliver to it is that of the possibility of the full realization of life in the energy of that Spirit. Our business is ever to urge men to call on the Name of the Lord, and thus to be delivered from the punitive activities of His judgment.

The whole message of the prophecy therefore insists, in common with the messages of all the prophets, upon the active sovereignty of God; and calls us to a recognition of the fact that every period is that of the Day of the Lord. To remember that is indeed to understand Kingsley's poem, and to live in the power of the truth it declares:

" The Day of the Lord is at hand, at hand!
    Its storms roll up the sky;
The nations sleep starving on heaps of gold;
    All dreamers toss and sigh;
The night is darkest before the morn;
When the pain is sorest the child is born,
    And the Day of the Lord at hand.

" Gather you, gather you, angels of God—
    Freedom, and Mercy, and Truth;
Come! for the Earth is grown coward and old;
    Come down, and renew us her youth.
Wisdom, Self-Sacrifice, Daring, and Love
Haste to the battlefield, stoop from above,
    To the Day of the Lord at hand.

" Gather you, gather you, hounds of hell—
    Famine, and Plague, and War;
Idleness, Bigotry, Cant, and Misrule,
    Gather, and fall in the snare!
Hireling and Mammonite, Bigot and Knave,
Crawl to the battlefield, sneak to your grave,
    In the Day of the Lord at hand.

" Who would sit down and sigh for a lost age of gold,
    While the Lord of all ages is here?
True hearts will leap up at the trumpet of God;
    And those who can suffer, can dare.
Each old age of gold was an iron age too,
And the meekest of saints may find stern work to do,
    In the Day of the Lord at hand."

II

THE VOICE OF JONAH

The Pity of God

SCRIPTURE LESSON: JONAH 3:4.
"Should not I have pity on Nineveh?"—JONAH 4:11.

WE have been living for the past half-century
or more in a philosophic atmosphere which
has created a certain attitude towards the
Book of Jonah. It is almost impossible now to open
the book and take a reading from it without people's
thoughts centering upon a fish! Men have been so
busy with the tape measure endeavoring to find the di-
mensions of the fish's belly that they seem to have had
no time to plumb the depths of the Divine revelation.
That is why we began our reading at chapter three. I
should be sorry if anyone imagined that I omitted the
first two chapters because I doubt their historic accuracy. My philosophy of God does not admit my doubting this, especially in view of the fact of a statement
concerning Him four times made in the course of the
book. "The Lord prepared a great fish," "The Lord
God prepared a gourd," "God prepared a worm," "God
prepared a sultry east wind." Thus with God behind
the fish, the gourd, the worm, the east wind, I find no
room for difficulty.

But I am far more concerned with what the book is intended to teach, and I believe that the whole thing flames and flashes in the seven words which I have selected as text:

"Should not I have pity on Nineveh?"

They were the words of God concerning a great city, and they were spoken to a man who knew God so well that he sinned against Him. Commissioned to go to Nineveh, he desired to escape from the responsibility, because he knew that if Nineveh repented, judgment would not fall upon it; and the one thing for which he was anxious was that Nineveh should be destroyed.

The book in itself is a revelation of heroism on the part of Jonah. It is not strictly a prophetic utterance, but rather a prophetic story. It was written for the people of God because they were guilty of the same sin, that of an exclusiveness that shut God out from all save their own national life. Jonah had to be brought into harmony with the facts concerning God through his own experience, and when this had taken place he was heroic enough to write the story of his own failure, and so warn the people against similar failure.

As we have said, these words of God concerned a great city. Many years ago Prince Bismarck said:

"Great cities are great sores upon the body politic," and I think no one will be prepared to challenge the accuracy of that declaration. According to the Biblical literature, the first city built was named Enoch, and it was built by a murderer. If from there we trace the history of cities in the Bible and outside the Bible, ending with this London of ours, notwithstanding its greatness and its grandeur, the statement is proven to be correct.

Nevertheless the city is the ultimate purpose of God for humanity. To refer once more to this Biblical literature, we find it opens in a garden, and closes in a city. The whole story from Genesis to Revelation is that of man's attempt to build a city. Having failed in the garden, rebelled against the one central Authority of the universe, he has been endeavoring to build cities, and so to realize the Divine intention, apart from the Divine order, and he has always failed.

In the midst of the history there passes before us in vision the city of Nineveh, having six-score thousand children, not knowing the difference between their right hand and their left. It was so great a city that it took three days to walk across it. God beheld that city, and knew its sin, and it is concerning it that He said:

"Should not I have pity on Nineveh?"

Thus we have a revelation of the Divine attitude towards a city outside the covenant of law, a city sinning against the light which Paul shows is ever shining in creation, a city which we know was saved from impending doom until it repented of its own repentance, when a hundred years later it was destroyed.

At the moment God, speaking to His messenger, reveals Himself in these arresting words:

"Should not I have pity on Nineveh?"

The whole emphasis of the enquiry should be placed upon the pronoun "*I*." Jonah, and the nation of which he was a member, had no thought of pity for Nineveh, and God was inquiring whether in their attitude they were thinking of Him from the same standpoint. The supreme word of Jonah to our age today is that of this voice, which raises this question, and answers it in the only way in which it can be answered, namely, that God does pity Nineveh.

Remembering then that the Church of God is the instrument in the world for the revelation of God, and that whatever the attitude of God is towards the cities of men, that should be the attitude of the Church; the question then with its inevitable answer reveals what is the attitude of God towards man, and towards the cities of men. It is never that of aloofness, or of distance. That was the sin of Judah. That was the sin of Jonah.

Gods knows the city. That of course is a general statement to which consent will be given. It is well to make it particular in application. God knew Nineveh. God knows London. More than fifty years ago Charles Kingsley said about London:

"God knows it. He knows the West with its tawdry splendor, its cultured indifference, its veneered rottenness, its throbbing heartache."

Though half a century has passed, would anyone care to alter that description of the West End? But Kingsley continued:

"And He knows the East with its grim fight with poverty, its vulgar cesspools of immorality, its unhealthy dwellings, its open shame, its smothered agony."

In these words he brought to our consciousness vividly an application of the truth that God knows. It is so in this regard also that:

"All things are naked and laid open before the eyes of Him with Whom we have to do."

The story of Jonah reveals another startling fact that we may express in the language of our own day by saying, God knows about the horses. The number of these is growing less on the streets of London. That does not alter the fact revealed in the statement that God saw the city of Nineveh, not only human beings, but also "much cattle."

That, however, has in it very little consolation. Mere knowledge can leave the heart indifferent, but here is a declaration not only revealing the knowledge of God, but declaring His care.

Faber truthfully sang:

> "There is no place where earth's sorrows
> Are more felt than up in Heaven.
> There is no place where earth's failings
> Have such kindly judgment given."

I think sometimes we are likely to forget that human conditions affect God, and that in the interest of humanity He is not impassive. He knows, He feels, He cares, He suffers, as well as rejoices. Some years ago a theologian of great ability, to whom some of us owe much, wrote a volume, the title of which was "The Impassive God." His arguments were all intended to show that God is not really affected by emotion in any form. When I read it I said, and I still say: Thank God that is not my God. The deeper truth is revealed in the statement that

> "In every pang that rends the heart,
> The Man of sorrows hath His part."

Many years ago one wrote:

"Over against His dead,
  God sat in silence; for the earth was dead,
    And dimly lay upon her awful bier,
  Wrapped round in darkness; yea, her shroud was wrought
    Of clouds and thunder; for the earth had died
  Not gently and at peace, as tired men die
    Towards the evening; but as one who dies
  Full of great strength, by sudden smiting down.
    The earth was dead, and laid upon her bier,
  And God, Sole Mourner, watched her day and night—
    The living God a Watcher by the dead,
  Sole Mourner in the Universe for her
    Who had been once so fair."

That is indeed a piteous and heart-rending picture.
But the writer did not stop there, but continuing sang:

"But, behold, there came
  One treading softly to the House of Death,
    Down from among the angels, through the room.
  He came as comes a King, unto the place
    Where lay the dead; and He laid His right hand
  Of strength on her, and called her tenderly,
    Saying, 'Arise, beloved, from thy sleep,
  For I will ransom thee by Death to Life;
    Arise and live.'"

There is light in that quotation for the argument we
are now considering. God cares for the suffering, the
dying, the dead world. All disability lies within the
consciousness of God, the dwellings of the people, the
workshops of men and women, all are under His sur-
veillance. The mental suffering of humanity, the misery of mystery, and the mystery of misery, and above

all, the spiritual death, which is lack of consciousness of eternal things. All that which Russell Lowell described as "the accursed mountain of sorrow" lies most heavily on the Divine heart. Whatever the conditions of men may be, or whatever their sin, the voice of God is heard saying, "Should not I have pity?"

Listening to that word we observe not only the fact of the knowledge of God, and that of His care, but the equally patent fact of His activity, sending His prophets, sending His Son, speaking to men in divers portions and divers manners, and then in full and final perfection in the Word. No problem has ever been too complex for His wisdom, no opposition too mighty for His power, no darkness too dense for His light, no trifle too trivial for His notice.

God has only found one difficulty, and that is the will of man. Humanity in its rebellion, in its stubbornness has lifted its puny fist and smitten the face of God. This rebellion might be dealt with as it would seem, by blotting humanity out; but God being what He is, cannot do this. We call to mind the word of the prophet to the ancient people of God: "How shall I give thee up?" It is against this attitude and activity of God that Jonah rebelled, and through discipline had to be brought into agreement therewith.

Returning to what has already been said, that the Church of God is in the world to represent God, we at once see our responsibility concerning the cities of men. As we look at the city today we find selfishness mastering its activities, covetousness as the passion of endeavor, and everywhere men acting upon the diabolical philosophy which believes only in the survival of the fittest. God is not in any such thinking, and the Church of God is called to take up and reveal the attitude of God, self-emptying instead of selfishness, sacrifice versus covetousness, and salvation for the unfit, instead of the survival of the fit.

Said the apostle, We seek a city, and he certainly did not intend to show that we were traveling towards Heaven, and hoping to arrive. The work of seeking the city is an earthly work. Setting the mind and affection on things above, we are to act in the midst of the things as they are.

The question will be asked: How is the Church of God to carry out this responsibility? First, by inward realization of the principles of the city of God, the city that lies foursquare, the city with its doors open to every point of the compass, the city characterized by translucent purity and radiant beauty.

From that standpoint of personal realization she is called upon to enter the corporate life of the city in which she lives. Whether a one-roomed dwelling is to be is a question, not of the landlord, but of the family; and the Church stands for that. The question of how many hours a day the factory is to be occupied by the sweating worker is not the question of the manufacturer's profit, but of the worker's health. Whether any given area is to have one drink shop or a hundred is the question of the well-being of the inhabitants, not of the dividends of the Trade. This means that the Church must be interested in men appointed to office in civic affairs. If our walls are ever to be salvation and our gates praise, our officers must be peace, and our exactors righteousness.

Necessarily this means that the Church must press forward constantly in her distinctive work of calling men and women into personal contact with God through Christ. The measure in which we are able to serve is the measure in which we sympathize with God. We remind ourselves again of that stated at the commencement, that Jonah's failure was due to the fact that he did not sympathize with God.

Our Lord Himself declared of Himself: "A Greater than Jonah is here," and the difference between Jonah and Jesus is exactly revealed. Both of them knew God. Jesus was in sympathy with God. Jonah was not. Jesus beheld the city and wept over it.

Thus the voice of Jonah to us today calls us not only to know God, but to be in sympathy with Him, to feel His pity, to carry out His activity, and to show to men what a God He really is.

III

THE VOICE OF AMOS

Famine for the Word of God

Scripture Lesson: Amos 1:1, 2; 7:12-16a; 8:1, 2 and 11-14.

"Behold, the days come, saith the Lord God, that I will send a famine in the land, not a famine of bread, nor a thirst for water, but of hearing the words of the Lord. And they shall wander from sea to sea, and from the north even to the east; they shall run to and fro to seek the word of the Lord, and shall not find it. In that day shall the fair virgins and the young men faint for thirst. They that swear by the sin of Samaria, and say, As thy God, O Dan, liveth; and, As the way of Beer-sheba liveth; even they shall fail, and never rise up again."—Amos 8:11-14.

AMID the galaxy of the Hebrew prophets, Amos has his own peculiarly radiant glory and beauty. Technically he was an untrained man. That is what he meant when he said to Amaziah: "I was no prophet, neither was I a prophet's son," the latter statement meaning that he had not studied in the school of the prophets. In the language of today, Amos was a layman. He was a herdman, a dresser of sycamore trees. He came from Tekoa, which was possibly in the southern kingdom of Judah. Actually he was indeed a prophet in the highest and only true sense of the word, for he said:

"The Lord took me from following the flock, and the Lord said unto me, Go, prophesy unto My people Israel."

Thus he is a brilliant example of the fact that a man who may have had no technical training may yet be a prophet of the Lord. His messages were redolent of the soil and the herd. His figures of speech were drawn from his calling. He was blunt and unconventional. We discover that as we remember that when he went to the court in Samaria, and addressed the men and women of the court, he described the latter as cows. We are liable not to be arrested by that fact, because we have rendered it, "Hear this word, ye kine of Basham."

No other prophet followed the method of Amos. Having come from Tekoa, he began to preach, and it is evident that he at once attracted attention. He began by denouncing surrounding nations. His first message was concerned with the far northeast, Damascus. Then turning his attention to the southwest, he dealt with Gaza. Once again he directed his words toward Tyre in the northwest. From there he spoke to Edom in the southeast. Then his message concerned Ammon in the east. Next he delivered a message concerning Moab in the southeast. Immediately following that he spoke to Judah, and finally came to deal with Israel, delivering the message for which all the previous ones constituted preparation.

He spoke of the cruelty of Damascus, of the traffic of the slave trade engaged in by Gaza, of the slave trade carried on by Tyre, of the unforgiving spirit of Edom, of cruelty based upon cupidity in Ammon, of the violent and vindictive hatred of other peoples by Moab. Coming to Judah, he denounced the nation because of its despising of the law of God. At last, dealing with Israel in his final message, that message was illuminated by all he had been saying to surrounding nations as he spoke of the corruption of the people who had known marvelous deliverances.

In reading the prophecy, it is noticeable that as long as Amos was talking in Israel, and denouncing surrounding nations, he was popular. That, we may say in passing, is always so. Today a man may denounce Germany, Italy, France, Russia, and arouse little resentment. It is when his message has to do with the home nation that his popularity is challenged. When Amos began to speak directly to Israel, Amaziah protested, advising him to leave the country.

The whole of his messages had a twofold significance. They reveal the fact that God maintained His government over all the nations, Damascus, Gaza, Tyre, Edom, Ammon, Moab. They also reveal the supreme fact that the responsibility of such nations is created by the measure of their privilege. He said nothing to any nation of such severity as the words he addressed to Israel. The Divine wrath in fulness was reserved for the nation of principal privilege.

The passage read as text is taken from the third section of the prophecy, in which Amos was pronouncing judgment upon Israel. He did that under a fourfold figure, first that of locusts, then that of fire, then of a testing plumb-line let down by the side of a wall, and finally the figure of the basket of summer fruit. It was revealed to him that that basket of summer fruit was intended to indicate that everything was indeed complete, that Israel had come to ripeness in iniquity, and God's judgment was inevitable. Under this final figure, indicating the imminence of coming judgment, the prophet employed these words, declaring the coming of a famine of hearing the words of the Lord.

Let it at once be observed that the statement does not refer to a capricious withholding on the part of God of His words to men. It rather indicates a condition of man in which he is incapable of hearing, of discerning, of knowing. The Word of the Lord may still be uttered. Prophets may still be speaking. The writings may still be read, but the people do not hear the voices. A famine of hearing the Word of the Lord describes a condition of life in which the message from the unseen is not heard. Humanity is unconscious of the voices from the unseen, which plumbs the deep necessity of the human heart; and consequently there is no authority which is unquestioned. That is a description of the people suffering from a famine of hearing.

The question immediately arises: How does such a condition come about? We find the answer in the statement:

"They that swear by the sin of Samaria, and say, As thy God, O Dan, liveth: and, As the way of Beersheba liveth; even they shall fail."

These northern people had substituted a false worship for the true. In olden days Jeroboam had set up calves to represent God, which of course utterly failed to do so; but the people were still swearing by them, as their gods. In other words, these people had substituted the creature for the Creator, and consequently rendered themselves incapable of hearing the Word of God. They had substituted something that had no value, that had no message, which did not come out of the unseen, and consequently failed to reach the depths of the human soul. They were devoting their lives to these false gods, and therefore could not hear the voice of God.

This always happens when man puts anything in the place of God. He becomes dull and insensate. God is still speaking, but he does not hear. There are those who profess to substitute Nature for God, and tell you they are worshiping Nature. There are those who substitute some form of priestism, or some ceremonial and ritual. In such cases, and all similar cases, men fail to hear the voice of God. The Bible ever becomes a sealed book when man turns from God. The result is famine of hearing the Word of God, and the issue of such famine is emaciated humanity.

The prophet then described what happens, and that in a most remarkable way. It issues inevitably in restlessness.

"They shall wander from sea to sea, and from the north even to the east; they shall run to and fro to seek the word of the Lord, and shall not find it."

Every attempt to satisfy life without God has this issue. This is the reason of all the restless feverishness which is so evident today. Watch the roads of England today, and the rushing of the motor-cars. Surely they wander from sea to sea, from north to east, backward and forward. Recently passing by the Welsh Chapel at Charing Cross, I saw on what is described as a wayside pulpit, these words:

"The place where you will arrive is more important than the speed at which you travel."

That is what seems to be forgotten. The speed is everything and the destination unknown.

Nevertheless the prophet says these restless people are seeking the Word of the Lord, and that very restlessness, if men did but recognize it, is a quest for God, but it is futile. What men are seeking is a God Who does not govern, and that means while sin is referred to, there is no consciousness of guilt, and the very principles upon which the universe is built are ignored.

All this is not confined to people who make no profession of godliness. It is discoverable within organized Church life, in the quest for new preachers, new movements, new theologies. Men are often so busy listening to these voices that they are in danger of not hearing the voice of God. The calf of Samaria is put up where God ought to be. Something mean, paltry, vanishing and destructive is where God ought to be; and the result is that there is a famine for hearing the Word of the Lord.

Continuing, the prophet said, they shall search and not find. Materialism is a perpetual lust. Sensualism is a deadly opiate. Novelty is a pernicious irritant. The human heart finds neither rest nor quietness in any of these. Restlessness is a symptom of fever, and fever is ever a destructive fire.

There is no famine of the Word of the Lord. The abridged report of the British and Foreign Bible Society for 1936 was entitled "The Flowing Tide." In that we learn that in the previous year the supply of Bibles exceeded in number any year known in the history of the Society. God is speaking, and is speaking through the Scriptures. They are being bought and scattered; and yet there is a famine for hearing the Word of God. It is possible to buy this Book, and read it, possible to study it, and yet never hear God.

When the prophet turned to describe the issue of the famine I am impressed with omissions. He did not say a single word about full-grown men and women. He said nothing concerning the aged. This does not of course mean that such are unaffected by the fact. The full-grown are tending to the arrest of development, and the cessation of work. The aged are moving towards the shadows, and have not long to continue. They undoubtedly are also suffering. But when the prophet spoke of results he took the young, the fair virgins and the young men, the strongest and the most hopeful and beautiful. He described life at its finest on the human level, and said of such, they shall "faint for thirst." Including all the things Amos did not refer to, we see what famine of hearing the Word of the Lord really means. The morning is overcast. The noon becomes a tempest. The night is starless. The finest capacities represented in the fair virgins and the young men, lacking true inspiration, fail and perish. That is the voice of the Hebrew prophet to our own age, and it is one which we need to hear as surely as did Israel in those far-gone centuries.

Standing back then from this remarkable book, the

first thing that impresses us is the fact that responsibility is commensurate with privilege. To Israel had been granted the light. Of them was the law, and the oracles of God. Therefore their responsibility was greater than that of Damascus, and that of any of the other nations referred to by Amos. I do not hesitate to say that no nation today has had greater privileges than we have, and that means that our responsibility is commensurately great. I think that perhaps the most hopeful sign of the present time is that there are evidences of the consciousness of ignorance. Everywhere men are inquiring: What is it we lack? They are saying that God does not seem to speak, and yet He is speaking all the time. I repeat that the fact that men are beginning to realize the fact is in itself a sign of hope.

Another fact of supreme importance is that the famine passes when men stop to listen. In that matchless story told by our Lord, which we call the story of the Prodigal, we have an account of a man who had come to the place of famine, and that because he had refused to submit to authority. Of him we read that something happened when he came to himself. It was when stripped to nakedness and reduced to the pangs of hunger that he became conscious first of his own personality. There was born within him a double conviction, that of his own dire necessity, and that of the amplitude of supply in the house of his father. Happy indeed is any man or woman who, coming there, goes further and says:

"I will arise, and go to my father."

The capacity for hearing is created in that attitude of return.

Another Hebrew prophet declares of God that He is "a God ready to pardon." The moment we set our faces back towards Him, we hear His voice speaking to the depths of our souls, and speaking with full and final authority. All I am saying has of course an individual application, but it is equally true nationally. In this nation there is still a famine of hearing the Word of the Lord. We have to go back to the old Mosaic word, reemphasized by Jesus in His use of it, as revealing the full and final philosophy of life:

"Man liveth not by bread alone; but by every word that proceedeth out of the mouth of God doth man live."

God is speaking. If men will wait and listen, whether the accents are often but a faint whisper, or of thunder, His voice will still be heard, and the famine will pass, and life become full and satisfied.

IV

THE VOICE OF HOSEA

Sin, Judgment, Love

SCRIPTURE LESSON: HOSEA 2:14-16; 6:1-4; 11:1-4, 8, 9; 14:4-8.

"Who is wise, and he shall understand these things? prudent, and he shall know them? for the ways of the Lord are right, and the just shall walk in them, but transgressors shall fall therein."
—HOSEA 14:9.

THESE words constitute an epilogue to the prophecy written unquestionably by Hosea himself. The period of his ministry in the Kingdom of Judah extended over seventy years, and, without any doubt, in this book we have his own condensation of the burden of his preaching during that period. Having completed his work he wrote:

"Who is wise, and he shall understand these things? prudent, and he shall know them? for the ways of the Lord are right, and the just shall walk in them, but transgressors shall fall therein."

The epilogue becomes all the more arresting from the fact that this is the only prophecy of the sixteen prophetic books which has such an epilogue. It is impossible to read the words without recognizing that the intention of the prophet was to challenge attention. It reveals the conditions upon which the writing may be studied, "Who is wise?" "Who is prudent?" The words *wise* and *prudent* are simple and beautiful words, but the actual words of the prophet are more arresting. Wisdom means having true light, and prudent signifies being gifted with the light. The one who has true light shall understand, consequently he who is gifted with the light shall know. The question which reveals conditions is followed by the impressive declaration "The ways of the Lord are right." The word "ways" is a Hebrew word signifying a road, that is, a course of action, and describes God's highways of movement. The prophet declared that these are right. He had in mind unquestionably all the effects of the Divine government and activity which he had been declaring, interpreting, and foretelling to the people.

He next revealed two attitudes towards this truth of the rightness of the ways of God. The first is that "the just shall walk in them," and the second, "transgressors shall fall therein." The ways of God remain unchanged, and are always right, and those who are obedient to them walk in them, that is, maintain the journey. On the other hand, those who are disobedient fall on the same highway.

In answer, therefore, to this challenge and declaration, we inquire, What are the ways of God declared to be right, as they are revealed in this prophecy? The answer is found as we catch the true significance of the messages delivered by Hosea, as we have said, over a period of seventy years. When we face the prophecy, making this inquiry, we may briefly summarize and declare that we find in it first a clear revelation of God's attitude towards sin, distinct affirmations concerning His activity in judgment upon sin, and su-

premely a declaration of the appeal of His love. Three
words, then, indicate the lines, namely, sin, judgment,
love. In every case these are dealt with from the
standpoint of the ways of God among, and for, His
people; His attitude toward sin, His activity in judgment, His appeal in love. These three things merge
into the perfect music of the prophecy. These three
things combine to make clear what are the ways of
God that the prophet declared to be right.

What, then, does Hosea teach us concerning sin?
First and foremost, that the sin of a people of high
privilege is the most heinous of which humanity is ca-
pable. That was the sin of Judah. God had loved them,
and had lavished His love upon them, and they had
answered that love with infidelity. It is noticeable that
in this prophecy certain vulgar forms of sin seem
hardly to be referred to. They are referred to, but are
employed in a moral and spiritual sense. Deeper down
than any of the sins which are venial is that of infidelity to love. In the case of Judah it was the sin of
a people who had been loved by Jehovah, found by
Jehovah, brought out of captivity by Jehovah. They
were a people whom God had taught to walk, and taken
them in His arms and loved them with a love passing
the love of woman. In spite of this they had been
unfaithful to their covenant with Him.

Hosea had learned the meaning of it by his own
broken heart. His own home life had been destroyed,
and he had passed through the intolerable agony
created by the infidelity of Gomer, the woman whom
he had loved. Through that experience he had learned

what sin really means, and that is why he adopted the strangely arresting and vulgar words to describe sin as adultery and harlotry. The sin of adultery is that of seeking satisfaction in unlawful relations. This is what these people had done. Harlotry is worse. It is the sin of prostituting high possessions for the sake of hire and gain. This also is what Judah had done. As the prophet declared, God had met them, loved them, taught them to walk, carried them in His arms, and they had gone after other gods.

Perhaps the supreme revelation at this point is that of God's attitude toward such sin. The first fact is that it caused suffering to the heart of God, and the second is that the holiness of God made impossible any condoning of such sin, or any compromise with it. The picture is graphic and terrible, but it was the truth concerning these people. They had contemned the law of God, and consequently violated His love. In tender and beautiful language God spoke to them:

"I will betroth thee unto Me for ever,"
thus indicating His purpose. They had, however, turned from Him, and had done despite to His love, as they had played the harlot and adulteress. The result was that God had suffered. Nevertheless there could be no condoning of the sin, and no compromise with it. He that is wise will understand. He that is prudent will know. The ways of the Lord are right, and His attitude toward sin is ever that of measuring it by its failure to respond to privilege.

We hear oftentimes in conversation references to

little sins and great sins. There is a sense in which any such distinction is entirely unwarranted. Yet there is another sense in which it is true, and if we take the national outlook which Hosea was taking, the sin of the people of privilege is far more terrible than that of people who have not had privilege. The shining of the light always creates responsibility. In the last analysis we may put it bluntly and say it were far better to have been born in the heart of Africa and never heard about God than to have been born in England, if we are untrue to God. This great prophecy, then, with its sob and its sigh, teaches us that God suffers when humanity treats Him as Gomer had treated Hosea.

But as we have twice already said, there can be no compromise with the sin, and no condoning of it. Therefore we find as clearly revealed the fact not only of God's attitude toward sin, but that of His necessary and inevitable activity in judgment. In this case we use the word judgment as indicating the punitive element in justice. Throughout this prophecy there are passages vibrant with the thunder of wrath. Nevertheless in the light of this prophecy, and indeed, in the light of the whole of the Biblical revelation, we discover that God's punishment of sin is never a capricious stroke. It is rather the irrevocable outworking of sin itself. God has so constituted the universe we live in, the moral universe, that we cannot escape from such results. Sin always results in judgment. "The wages of sin is death." "Be not deceived, God is not mocked; whatsoever a man soweth that shall he also reap."

That means quite clearly that he reaps what he has sown. God's government has provided that a punishment is inevitable, included in the course of sin.

Nevertheless, God never abandons man at that point, and as we listen to Hosea and recognize that the irresistible compulsion of His government compels the outworking of sin to the final issue, there is yet much more to be said. There can be no escape from the fact of the government of God. When the Psalmist inquired, "Whither shall I go from Thy presence?" the complete answer is found in the declaration that it cannot be done. There is no place where God is not, and there is no place where His government is not in full force. No man can escape from God, and no man can put his life outside His government. It is quite true that we pray for the coming of His Kingdom, and rightly so, but there is a sense in which all men are in the Kingdom of God. Their experience of that Kingship depends upon their attitude to God. A man can rebel against Him. He can fling himself against the bosses of His mighty shield and be broken by the impact; or he can shelter in His heart and be shielded from all harm. By that government God is ever compelling man to work out to its ultimate issue his thinking, his choosing, his philosophy. When Isaiah asked: "Who is this?" as he looked upon the Warrior, in answer he employed an arresting figure of speech. He was treading the wine-press, that is, compelling the grapes to yield up their own life, and their own nature. God is ever doing this, and He is doing it with the nations today. Man everywhere, under the pressure of the Divine government, is compelled to work out to its ultimate conclusion his own philosophies and choices.

Judgment, then, as punishment, is never first the will of God. It is rather the willing of man, and then the fact of the will of God encompassing human will and so carrying out the principles of the moral universe. The penalties of sin are as irrevocable as are the blessings of righteousness. "The ways of the Lord are right."

And now we come to this supreme fact that all the way through we hear the appeal of the love of God. That really is the dominant note of Hosea's message. It thrills to the tireless music of a Psalm. This love of God was unveiled to Hosea through his own tragedy. Gomer had deceived him, had been unfaithful to him, and had left him bereft, and his heart broken as she had gone after her false lovers. The historic story reveals the fact that her lovers had forsaken her, and she had been reduced to the position of a slave. While in that condition Hosea was commanded to seek her, and in order to gain her, he had to buy her as a slave. In doing that he opened a door of hope for her in the Valley of Achor. The word Achor signifies troubling, and so the door of hope was opened in the valley of troubling. Through this personal and poignant experience God was revealing to Hosea what He was prepared to do with a nation that had been guilty of spiritual adultery and harlotry. Out of the valley of trouble there opened a door of hope. It is a love-song that passes all human understanding. Hosea only came to appreciate it when, in obedience, he did the very things that he was commanded.

Again we hear the same love message in the words:

"The Lord . . . hath torn, and He will heal us;
He hath smitten, and He will bind us up."

That great cry was wrung out of the heart of the anguish of God in the presence of the rebellion of His people. Ephraim in infinite scorn was described as a cake not turned, doughy and flaccid, and uncooked on one side, and burnt to a cinder on the other. Nevertheless we hear the cry of the Divine heart:

"How shall I give thee up, Ephraim?"

And the answer is described presently as again we hear the voice of God saying:

"I will heal their backsliding, I will love them
freely."

Thus we listen to a veritable anthem out of the heart of God.

That is why, in my selection of readings as a preface to this meditation, I chose those which I did. I might have selected other passages, stern and terrible denunciations, which are all there, revealing the nature of sin, and the inevitable judgment. But I chose those in which this love-song is constantly heard.

These are the permanent notes of this great message of Hosea, and it is well that we remember that in spite of this final thought of the love of God, we must not emphasize one note apart from the others, and so minimize the value of the whole. If we listen to the love-song and forget the declarations of judgment, we are false to God. If we emphasize the fact of judgment and forget the love-song, we blaspheme against God.

Sin in the last analysis, in its most terrible form, is infidelity to love. It hurts God. It destroys the sinner. He can never condone sin, but He can and does redeem the sinner. "Who is wise?" he will understand. "Who is prudent?" he will know.

V

THE VOICE OF OBADIAH

The Kingdom Shall Be the Lord's

SCRIPTURE LESSON: OBADIAH.

*"And saviours shall come up on Mount Zion to judge the mount of Esau; and the Kingdom shall be the Lord's.—*OBADIAH 21.

THE prophecy of Obadiah is admittedly a strange page in the Old Testament. One could almost imagine it being said that surely there is no message in it for us, and for our times. Nevertheless it is true that Isadore said of this prophecy in his book on the Allegories of the Sacred Scriptures:

"Among all the prophets, he is the briefest in number of words; in the grace of mysteries he is their equal."

The book really consists of one set message. The identity of the prophet and the historic setting are of minor importance. It is impossible to say with any definiteness who Obadiah was. We meet the name in other places in Scripture, but we cannot identify him. Neither can the actual hour of his prophesying be fixed. Therefore we do not pause with these minor matters, but give attention to the message itself.

The peculiar quality of the book is that in it the antagonism between Jacob and Esau is brought into clearer view than in any other of the prophetic writings. If we look at the first eight verses we shall find that much that Obadiah is recorded as saying is found in the prophecy of Jeremiah, which may mean that Obadiah was familiar with Jeremiah's prophecy, or that Jeremiah was familiar with Obadiah's prophecy.

This antagonism is patent throughout the Bible in definite historic statement and in continuous suggestion. In Genesis we read that "the children struggled within her." The fact thus stated created a premonition on the part of Rebekah which was most significant as it filled her with fear. A statement with which we are all familiar, "Jacob have I loved, Esau have I hated," seems to have given pause to very many thoughtful people. Let it at once be said that God's attitude did not create that in Jacob which He loved, or that in Esau which He hated. These men did not become what they were because God loved or hated. Rather it is true that God's love or hatred resulted from what they were, and what their character was. The antagonism was always recognized in the Old Testament, and emerges again in the New Testament, and is finally revealed in an almost startling way in two outstanding personalities, those of Jesus and Herod. We must remember that Herod was an Edomite, and Jesus according to the flesh was a descendant of Jacob. It is a very arresting and appalling fact that Jesus never spoke to Herod. He once sent him a stinging message, asserting His own authority, and the definiteness of His antipathy, dismissing him with profound contempt.

In this prophecy of Obadiah the background is Jacob. He is seen suffering, and suffering by the chastening hand of God; while in the foreground Esau is seen gloating over the suffering of Jacob, adding to his trouble; and God is seen dealing with both.

The supreme value of the revelation of Edom is that of concrete godlessness. We are far away from the days of Jacob and Esau, but the principles revealed in Jacob and Esau are still appearing, and indeed were never more manifest in human history than they are today. The two ideals, the two conceptions, the two methods of life are in the world still.

In this prophecy we have brought before us first of all, and principally, an unveiling of the spirit of Esau, and the meaning of Edom. The prophet was dealing with these things as they were manifested at the time, not in the individual men, but in the races descended from them.

What, then, is the revelation that we have here of Esau and Edom? It is a terrible picture of cruelty and violence. Edom is here seen watching, from her heights of self-satisfaction, the suffering of the nation of Israel as it was passing through the chastisements of God. Edom is revealed as looking on, and presently crossing the border-line, and acting so as to add to the suffering of Jacob.

That, however, is not the beginning of the revelation. What is the profound wrong which is revealed? If we say, as we have said, that it was that of godlessness, let us remember that there was something prior to that, and causing it. It is found in the words, "The pride of thine heart hath deceived thee." Pride of heart expressed itself in carelessness about God. There are some scholars who hold that the Edomites not only did not acknowledge God, but that they had no gods. Other nations had gods, but were idolaters. The Edomites seem to have done away with any reference to God or to gods in any form. "The pride of thine heart hath deceived thee." That is to say, they did not feel that God was a necessity in any sense.

When we come into the New Testament we encounter that tremendous phrase describing Esau, and applicable to all his descendants, and the attitude of life which he represented, "that profane person Esau." Profane here does not refer to careless or lewd speech. It means, quite literally, against the temple. The profane person is one who has no spiritual conception, whose life is that of pure materialism. The man who says, I do not want God; I am independent of God; that is pride of heart.

If that conception does not shock us it is because in our thinking today we have come to lay emphasis on certain sins, and shudder when we hear of them, failing to recognize that underlying all sin there is this root sin, the pride of heart that says this life is sufficient in itself, without any relationship to God.

That pride expressed itself in Edom as she climbed to the height of rocky fastnesses and said, "Who shall bring me down?" Mounting high as the eagle, making her nest among the stars, she was guilty of self-deification. The whole thing is illustrated by the fact of the case at the time of this prophecy. The Edomites were living in a rocky district which we have now come to call Petra, and they felt that their position was absolutely invincible. Moreover, it was a long time before anyone was able to break through their fastnesses and overcome them. They were the very embodiment then of practical defiant godlessness, expressing itself in the deification of self, and the conviction that self was sufficient, and that the fastnesses which it had made for its own protection were enough to protect it against all opposition.

We now inquire how was that pride of heart manifested? The one sin that is named as resulting from it was that of violence, cruelty, hardness of heart, opposition to everything that Jacob represented. It manifested itself first in passive cruelty. In the day of disaster they looked, and the day of destruction they rejoiced in. In the day of distress they vaunted themselves, and spoke proudly. Presently that which was passive became active. In the actual day of calamity they entered the gate, they looked upon the affliction, they robbed Jacob of his substance, and they cut off his escape when he endeavored to escape. All this is the expression of an attitude toward man which is the outcome of an attitude toward God. When God is ignored, violence is done to our fellow-men.

The question arises, How will this end? And it was in order to answer this, probably, that the prophet uttered his message. In that particular hour Jacob is revealed as depressed, suffering not only as the result of the chastisements of God, but from the brutal and violent opposition of Edom. Jacob heard that insolent cry of Edom. "Who shall bring me down?" and it seemed that the challenge had no answer, that Edom was always to flourish, that godlessness must perpetually remain in the ascendant. To that the reply is given in the words of Jehovah, "I will bring thee down," I will "destroy the wise men," I will dismay the "mighty men."

The prophet then shows that such action will be through the coöperation of events. The message to Edom was that "the men of thy confederacy" will be against you. "The men that were at peace with thee," that is under the covenant, will break their covenant. The men that are eating thy bread will become thine enemies. Thus, by coöperation of events under the government of God, Edom is to be brought down from her rocky fastnesses, and from her nest among the stars; and this issue will be what we sometime speak of as poetic justice.

"As thou hast done, it shall be done unto thee."

Then we come to the last word which is certainly an arresting and remarkable one.

"Saviours shall come up on mount Zion to judge the mount of Esau; and the Kingdom shall be the Lord's."

That final sentence seems as though it were an outburst from the depths of the heart, as the result of profound conviction, "The Kingdom shall be the Lord's." The statement that there shall be saviours on the mount of Zion is open to two interpretations. Much depends upon the meaning of the word "judge." "Saviours shall come up on mount Zion to judge the mount of Esau."

The prime meaning of this word *judge* is that of government in righteousness. Of course it often refers to that action of government which is punishment. To me at least there ever seems to shine in the statement of the prophet hope even for Esau, hope even for the godless; "saviours" on mount Zion, the hill of God, and there, if Esau so will, a judgment that deals with everything that is wrong, and sets it right, until at last "the kingdom shall be Jehovah's."

This last sentence in the prophecy is in harmony with all the prophetic writings. It cannot be too often emphasized that no Hebrew prophet ended on a note of pessimism. These men saw the gloom and the darkness, saw the iniquity and the godlessness, but they saw beyond. None of them saw everything ended in gloom and darkness and godlessness. They looked through, and this prophet in his brief message, in which he has shown us clearly the antagonism between godlessness and godliness, utters as his last word: "The Kingdom shall be the Lord's." He saw beyond the present conflict, beyond the suffering of Jacob, and the taunting of Edom, and the judgment that must inevitably come upon Edom, an hour in which all these things should end, and the kingdom should be Jehovah's.

This is the declaration that we need to hear and heed today. Perhaps godlessness was never more rampant and blatant than it is in this hour. The old days of infidel attack upon the Christian religion have largely passed away; and yet there never was a day when practical godlessness was more rampant than it is now.

Men are saying in effect: We do not need God. We have made our nest among the stars. Who will bring us down? Men are acting as independent of God, and therefore without prayer. They have no vision of the unseen, and no spiritual conception.

Yet in this very hour when men are taking up this attitude, all their confederacies and their self-sufficiency are working together towards the bringing of them down from the position of pride, that they may stand face to face with reality.

In spite of all these things, we affirm with Obadiah our conviction that "the Kingdom shall be Jehovah's." We are sure of it first because it is His today. He is reigning. The world has never escaped from the grasp or the grip of the government of God. There are so many things that we cannot understand today, but the one absolute certainty is that all these things are under the government of God. The fact remains, then, that the Kingdom shall be His because in this sense it is already His.

It is being made His in the full sense of human realization, because of His proclaimed Word and Gospel.

> "Though a wide compass round be fetched,
>   That what began best, can't end worst."

"The Kingdom shall be the Lord's."

The question arises as to where we stand in relation to this fact? Are we with Jacob or with Esau? Jacob was not a very praiseworthy person, but he represents us, and that is why he stands out so clearly, blundering, failing, foolish, but always believing in God even in the hours of his folly when he did stupid things. God was patient with him because of that fact, gave him a vision when he was wandering from his home through his own duplicity, and met him on his way back, crippling him in order to make him.

But am I with Esau, the profane person against the temple, having no vision of the unseen, no sense of the spiritual, satisfied in rocky fastnesses as I imagine, and crying out, "Who will bring me down?" If that is where I live, I must remember first that an alternative is before me. God is waiting, and He has provided a Saviour. The profane can be made sacred in the gracious economy of God. The final word, however, the only word with which to close this meditation, is the word of the prophet, with its vastness of meaning, and its application to individual life. "The Kingdom shall be the Lord's."

VI

THE VOICE OF MICAH

The Requirements of God

SCRIPTURE LESSON: MICAH 6:1-8.

"He hath shewed thee, O man, what is good; and what doth the Lord require of thee, but to do justly, and to love mercy, and to walk humbly with thy God?"—MICAH 6:8.

THE prophet Micah was contemporary with Isaiah. The burden of the three messages which he delivered was that of authority. He spoke principally to the cities as centers of national life, as having within them those who were exercising authority. He denounced in no measured terms the false rulers who were leading the people astray, and foretold in some of the most glorious sentences of the Old Testament literature of the coming of the one true Ruler. His messages were of course national in their first application, but in the words we have selected we find an individual note. The text constitutes the answer to an inquiry found in the two previous verses.

It is the inquiry of some soul in spiritual and moral trouble, one who evidently had passed under the influence of the prophetic teaching, was conscious of sin, and realized the personal note of responsibility.

"Wherewith shall I come before the Lord, and bow myself before the high God?"

Moreover the inquirer suggests possible ways of approach to God.

"Shall I come before Him with burnt offerings, with calves of a year old? Will the Lord be pleased with thousands of rams, or with ten thousands of rivers of oil?"

Then, rising to an appalling height to which in pagan darkness the soul of man often did rise, he cried:

"Shall I give my firstborn for my transgression, the fruit of my body for the sin of my soul?"

It was to this cry that the prophet replied.

If we look a little further back in the narrative we find that inquiry was the result of a plea which God was uttering to the nation,

"O My people, what have I done unto thee? and wherein have I wearied thee? testify against Me. For I brought thee up out of the land of Egypt, and redeemed thee out of the house of bondage; and I sent before thee Moses, Aaron, and Miriam."

Said God to the people, What have I done to you that you are weary of Me? It was the plaintive cry of a father's heart. It was in answer to that appeal that the cry of the afflicted soul was heard; and to that cry the prophet answered in these words.

All national affairs are finally reduced to individual application. Thus while the prophet delivered his messages to the nation failing in the matter of their authority, and foretold the coming of the true Authority, he made this individual statement. In that way we propose to consider it.

As we do so there are three things which arrest our attention, first a central assumption revealed in the words, "What doth the Lord require of thee?" the assumption evidently being that God does require. The second matter is the statement with which the text opens, "He hath shewed thee, O man, what is good"; the declaration that God has not left man without revelation as to His requirements. Finally, the whole text reveals what it is that God does require, and is an interpretation of goodness. It is "to do justly, to love mercy, and to walk humbly with thy God." Thus the prophetic message breaks itself up naturally and simply. Let us follow these lines.

First then, the great assumption. The individual note is very strong: "O man," in thy loneliness, the loneliness of thine own personality, shutting out all others for the moment from the consideration. The question is what God requires; and moreover, what thy God requires of thee? There is, as a matter of fact, something of infinite comfort and strength in that fact of address to personality. If God requires of a man, He is the God of that man.

Let us think of the justness of that claim that God does require. Man is not left to himself in the moral universe in which he lives. Necessarily we are assuming the authority of the Biblical revelation of God and the universe. If we merely think of God as an abstraction, or as a possibility, there is no meaning in our text. That is true of the whole Bible. We remind ourselves then of things with which we are familiar from childhood. God is the Creator. God is the King. God is the Father. God is the Redeemer.

God is Creator, and in that fact we discover the fundamental justness of the claim that He requires. If it were possible that we should create anything, which of course is not possible—we can make, but not create —we should inherently feel we had a right to expect from that which we created that for which it was created. Paul has expressed the whole matter by quotation, by the way, from the Old Testament, in clear language when he said:

"Shall the thing formed say to Him that formed it, Why didst Thou make me thus?"

But He is more than Creator. He has not created the world and cast it out to drift; and He has not created man and left him to himself. He is King, and so Law-giver, and His law conditions the being and authority of that which He has created. He requires, and that is the very essence of law.

But God is revealed as more than Creator and Lawgiver, He is Father. That word connotes His providence, His care, His watchfulness over that which He has created. His law is ever the expression of His love, and His Fatherhood is the proof of His watchfulness.

And yet something else has to be said. He is more than Creator, more than King, more than Father; He is Redeemer. His is the love that alters not when it alteration finds. His is the love that never fails. When there was no eye to pity, His eye pitied, and when there was no arm to save, His arm brought salvation.

When these facts are recognized, they all emphasize the fact that He has a right to require. His origination in creation is reasoned and purposeful. There is no human life which in the final analysis is not a Divine creation. We recognize the tremendous fact of procreation, but that has only to do with the physical side of personality. In itself it is a tremendous and awe-inspiring capacity; but it is of the utmost importance that we recognize that no baby born into the world whether, to speak in the terms of our human conditions, properly born or improperly born, but that there is in the creation of that personality an action of Deity. We have had fathers of our flesh, and that is all they were. God is the Father of spirits, and within every human personality there are to be found potentialities and possibilities far greater than those inherited from human forebears. The appalling fact of human nature today is that in its thinking of itself it has fallen to low levels. When Christ spoke of the necessity for the de-nial of self, He declared that when self is denied, self is sound. It is the false self that is to be denied. Re-generation is the re-birth of personality in order to the realization of the original Divine intention.

This is a moral universe. Vast tides of immorality seem to submerge the race, but in the last analysis, under the creative purpose and kingly authority of God, it remains moral. In other words, God requires.

We turn now to what is in some senses the amazing declaration of the text. In answer to the poignant cry of the soul in its sense of the necessity for coming to God,

"He hath shewed thee, O man, what is good."
We need to bear in mind that the first application of that was to the Hebrew people, and that the prophet here was really making a quotation from their law. In Deuteronomy we find these words:

"And now, Israel, what doth the Lord thy God require of thee, but to fear the Lord thy God, to walk in all His ways, and to love Him, and to serve the Lord thy God with all thy heart and with all thy soul."

The thing was written in the law given to the people, and consequently the prophet could say to the individual inquirer, "He hath shewed thee."

But we are gathered in days when the words have yet more powerful meaning. The good has been revealed not in a written law merely, but in an Incarnation. Jesus has been seen, proclaimed, and is known. In Him God has shown us what is good. It is well to remember that however varied may be our opinions even concerning the Person of Jesus, His goodness is universally recognized. Thus we have seen in Him what is good.

Yet once more, turning from those two applications, first to the Hebrew people in the law, and the second to the world through Incarnation, we remember that there are those who do not know the ancient law, and who have not even heard about Jesus Christ. Can the words of the text apply in any sense to such? It will be remembered that in the prologue to his Gospel, John referred to a light that lighteth every man. That light antedates the historic Incarnation, and is discovered where neither the law nor the Gospel has ever been proclaimed. There is that in human personality which was described by the writer of the Proverbs when he said, "The spirit of man is the lamp of the Lord." Let it be carefully observed that the statement is not a reference to the Spirit of God, but to the spirit of man. Thus, in the mystery of human personality there is a universal consciousness of good.

We turn to consider the suggestiveness of the word *good*. The word in our language is a great word, and has many applications. The Hebrew word employed has also many applications. It is used of well as opposed to ill, of beauty as opposed to ugliness, of strength as opposed to weakness, of right as opposed to wrong. There is no human being who is not able to make these distinctions. To admit illness is to recognize health. To know ugliness is to admit beauty. To refer to weakness is to admit the consciousness of strength. To face wrong is to consent to right as a possibility. Thus no man is without that light in measure, and it may at once be said that every man is responsible for the measure of his light, and for no more.

Finally the text gives us an interpretation of goodness. God is not requiring burnt offerings, calves of a year old, thousands of rams, or ten thousands rivers of oil, nor the fruit of the body for the sin of the soul. None of these things would have any value as offering to God as a means of approach to Him. Goodness is then revealed in the words, "to do justly, to love mercy, and to walk humbly with God." This is an arresting and indeed marvelous analysis of human life when it is good. Three things are named: doing justly, loving mercy, walking humbly with God. In these we discover first human relationship, doing justly, loving mercy; and then life is seen in its Divine relationship, walking humbly with God.

On consideration it is self-evident that the supreme thing is the last one named, walking humbly with God. When that is done the first two follow inevitably, doing justly and loving mercy in the midst of human relationships; and indeed, the phrases marking those human relationships again should be considered in the reverse order. Thus the true sequence for understanding is found if we take the threefold word, and work back; walking humbly with God, loving mercy, and doing justly. That is the full and final description of goodness.

However we will take them in the order in which we find them in the text. Goodness is first doing justly. We inquire: What is it to do justly? And we remind ourselves that the word so rendered comes from the great Hebrew word *mishpat*, which ultimately means justice. Justice requires first of all a righteous standard, secondly the finding of a true verdict, thirdly coming to a right decision, and finally, action in harmony with these things. To do justly in our dealings with men we must have a true standard, a righteous law. We must be careful that the decision we come to about our fellow man is a true one. We must be careful that our decisions concerning each person are just, and that our action is in harmony with the great, eternal principles found in the character of God. There is nothing harsh about the suggestion. It is pure, it is holy. It reveals the standard of ethical life, and in that sense I would go so far as to say that what the world needs more than anything else is justice in action.

Then we have the second suggestion in the words,

"to love mercy." The word for mercy is a great word, representing the idea of stooping, bending, serving, all activity created by love.

Let us carefully observe here a simple matter, which is nevertheless an important one. We are not told we are to love justice and do mercy. It is possible for a man to love justice in the abstract, and yet do unjust things to his fellow man. To love justice thus in the abstract is not enough. We are to do it. Moreover to do mercy is not enough. Again there may be a certain activity of what is called charity which does not spring from the deepest intention of the life. When mercy is loved, it is because the soul is in harmony with the compassions of God.

When we bring life to the test of this great statement, surely we are inclined to cry out: Who is sufficient for these things? It is this sense of insufficiency which causes the cry: "Wherewith shall I come before the Lord?" and the answer must begin at the close: By walking humbly with God. He ever loves mercy and does justly. When we are walking with Him in submission and fellowship we too shall love mercy and do justice.

We end this meditation on the message of Micah by reminding ourselves that we find no Gospel in that. It is rather a law. When our Lord said, "I am the light," we must remember that light can only condemn.

Nevertheless in these words of Micah there is a revelation of an overwhelming need for a Gospel, and the Gospel declares that Jesus is far more than light: He is life, and the Life-giver. If the declaration of the old

Hebrew prophet reveals to us our failure, the revelation that came by Jesus Christ shows the possibility of recovery and realization. He receives us. He renews us. He makes possible what God requires.

VII

THE VOICE OF NAHUM

The Vengeance of God

SCRIPTURE LESSON: NAHUM 1:1-15.

"The Lord is a jealous God and avengeth; the Lord avengeth and is full of wrath; the Lord taketh vengeance on his adversaries, and he reserveth wrath for his enemies."—NAHUM 1:2.

ROBERT WILLIAM DALE, the great preacher and theologian of a generation ago, said to me one day that he had known one man that he felt had a perfect right to talk about Hell, and that man was D. L. Moody. He stated that the reason that he so felt was that he never heard Moody refer to Hell without tears in his voice.

It is impossible to read this prophecy of Nahum without an almost frightening sense of awe. The very first sentence, which is hardly a sentence, but rather a descriptive phrase, introduces us to the subject of the book. It reads: "The burden of Nineveh," or as the marginal reading gives it with more accuracy, "The oracle concerning Nineveh."

The book of Nahum is the complement of the book of Jonah. One hundred years separate them. Nahum was a prophet who came to speak to the people of God in an oracle concerning Nineveh. The story of the book when Nahum uttered his message was prediction, that of the utter destruction of a great city and a great

71

people by the will and act of God. As we read the book we are reading what has become history. All the things that he uttered predictively have literally come to pass. The name of the prophet is suggestive, meaning comfort, and undoubtedly the purpose of his message was to bring comfort to Israel. At the time the nation was threatened by Assyria and by Nineveh, and Nahum revealed what was the Divine attitude towards Nineveh, and predicted the action wherein and whereby it should be blotted out as a city and a people.

So completely has this been fulfilled, that armies have actually marched over the city of Nineveh, ignorant of the existence of its ruins beneath. The message which Nahum delivered is closely compacted, clear in statement, logical in argument, definite in all its declarations.

At the commencement he described it as a vision: "The book of the vision of Nahum the Elkoshite." It is a vision of Jehovah from beginning to end, first a vision of Him in anger, and then of Him acting in vengeance. In this case we may take the chapter divisions as indicating the movement of the message. Chapter one deals with the verdict of vengeance, chapter two with the vision of vengeance, and chapter three with the vindication of vengeance.

The permanent value of the book is that in it we have an explanation of the anger of God, as it reveals the facts of that anger, the reason for it, and describes its activity. It is well to say at the beginning that as we read it we find it is touched all through with the light of tenderness and compassion. Those deep truths concerning the Divine nature are never lost sight of, even though His anger and wrath are being revealed.

This is in harmony with the revelation of God in the Bible, in its entirety. All the prophets spoke of the wrath of God in some form or another. All saw that God deals with certain aspects of life in vengeance, but in every one of them is found also the note which reveals His love and His tenderness. Any careful examination of these writings, and especially of this book, will show in the last analysis that the reason for the anger of God is found in His love.

Leaving every other reference we come face to face with the Lord Himself. There are many people who think of Him only in the way in which the children's hymn describes Him:

"Gentle Jesus, meek and mild."

Now, while that is perfectly true concerning Him, it is not all the truth. No prophet in the Old Testament said things so startlingly severe as Jesus did. He said, for instance, concerning those whom we teach to sing that hymn, that rather than offend a little child it would be profitable that a millstone should be hanged about the neck, and that we should be drowned in the depths of the sea. He was "gentle Jesus, meek and mild," for He loved the child, and He loved it so much that He declared—mark His word—that it would be profitable to be drowned in the depths of the sea rather than to cause it to stumble. It was Jesus Who beheld a city, and wept over it, but while those tears were still upon His face, He pronounced its doom:

"Behold, your house is left unto you desolate."

If we take the first eight verses of the prophecy we shall find a remarkable gathering together of words that reveal the truth about God as Nahum saw it. Each prophet had some distinct vision of God, and we can only know anything approaching the full truth concerning Him as we find the merging of these varied visions into that of the majesty of His Being. Isaiah saw Him lifted on His Throne while His train filled the temple. Ezekiel saw Him in the ancient symbolism of the East in the turning wheels and the living creatures. Jeremiah saw Him in wrath, and yet revealed His heart as he said: Oh that my head were a fountain of waters that I could weep for the sins of my people. Nahum saw Him, and the vision is revealed in these opening verses in which we have a remarkable collection of words. Let us first group them. "Jealous," "avengeth," "wrath," "anger," "indignation," "fierceness," "fury."

Now it is an arresting fact that in those opening sentences we find every word suggesting anger which is found in the Hebrew Bible. Let us further pause to briefly examine these words. The root idea of "jealousy" is that of intense emotional disturbance. It is wholly subjective. Jealousy is always the outcome of wrath, resulting from wrong done to love. It is an emotional revolt against infidelity.

Closely allied is the next word, "avengeth." That is no longer merely emotional, it is volitional, it is active. Vengeance, however, speaks of retribution, never of retaliation. Retribution and retaliation are not the

THE VOICE OF NAHUM

same. Man's anger almost always expressed itself in retaliation, God's never. His anger is retributive.

"Wrath" is the translation of a word which in the Hebrew simply means crossing over from one side to another. The wrath of God speaks of a change created in His attitude and activity. The prophetic declaration will be remembered that judgment is God's "strange act," that is to say, it is foreign to His heart, to His desire, to His purpose, to His intention, but there are conditions upon which such wrath is inevitable.

Then we have two words closely united here, "anger" and "indignation," each of them expressing activity, and indicating the expression of wrath.

Two others are closely allied, "fierceness," which means burning, and "fury," which is heat.

Now all this is certainly mechanical and technical, but in it we have a description of God, and that is of Jehovah, which is the word used by the prophet throughout. This name of God reveals Him as bending to the level of human necessity, and it is this God Who under certain conditions is moved to wrath, and acts in anger.

Now we examine this a little more particularly. In the second verse we have a threefold description, which is followed by a threefold exposition in verses six to eight. The description:

"The Lord is a jealous God and avengeth."
That describes passion in action.

"The Lord avengeth and is full of wrath."
—which is the same thing from the other side; that is,

it refers to an action that comes out of passion.   Then the final declaration:

> "The Lord taketh vengeance on His adversaries,
> and He reserveth wrath for His enemies."

It is clear from this threefold declaration that the wrath of God becomes active as the result of the passion that lies beyond it; and, moreover, that the action is always discriminative.

Then the prophet gave us an interpretation.   He began by the declaration:

> "The Lord is slow to anger, and great in power,
> and will by no means clear the guilty."

He then employed figurative language of the most intense character.   "The Lord hath His way in the whirl-wind."   The answer of God is seen as irresistible. Then notice carefully the declaration:

> "The Lord is good, a Stronghold in the day of
> trouble; and He knoweth them that put their trust
> in Him.   But with an overrunning flood He will
> make a full end of the place thereof,"

the reference being to Nineveh.

What, then, do we find revealed?   First, that the wrath of God is a passion born of love which proceeds to action.   As we continue our reading of the prophecy we see what Nineveh was in itself, and what Nineveh had been doing.   She had become hated of all the surrounding peoples because of her oppressive tyranny. In overbearing insolence she had resorted to every form of cruelty.   God heard the cry of the prisoner, and His anger against Nineveh was born of His love for those whom Nineveh had oppressed.   Nevertheless, He is slow to anger, and Nineveh was a proof of it. A hundred years before, when the reluctant prophet Jonah had gone to it, and had delivered a message of doom, and Nineveh had repented, God had waited. In the meantime Nineveh had committed that heinous sin of repenting of her repentance, and continued in her courses of cruelty. On account of that the wrath of God was active against Nineveh.

The prophet then gives his vision of that wrath of God in its activity. The reason for His anger is revealed in the words:

"There is one gone forth out of thee, that imagineth evil against the Lord, that counselleth wickedness."

That was a direct historic reference to Sennacherib. Full particulars regarding his action will be found by reference to the prophecy of Isaiah. That was the sin of Nineveh, as focused in Sennacherib, on the Godward side.

The results were patent in the city itself. In the third chapter we read:

"Woe to the bloody city! it is all full of lies and rapine; the prey departeth not. The noise of the whip, and the noise of the rattling of wheels; and prancing horses, and jumping chariots; the horsemen mounting, and the flashing sword, and the glittering spear; and a multitude of slain, and a great heap of carcases; and there is no end of the corpses, they stumble upon their corpses; because of the multitude of the whoredoms of the fell-favored harlot, the mistress of witchcrafts, that selleth nations through

her whoredoms, and families through her witchcrafts."

It was because of this that Jehovah said: "Behold, I
am against thee." God is seen, then, as angry because
the ruler of a people had lifted himself against the will
of God, and this had produced the brutalizing effect
upon the people, so that they had become oppressive
and cruel, bringing misery and destruction wherever
they came. Thus the anger of God was in the interests
of others, those who were oppressed, those who were
downtrodden, those who were wronged. Let us repeat
that the anger of God became active against this city
after long patience, and when the case had become
hopeless:

"There is no assuaging of thy hurt, thy wound
is grievous."

The cup of iniquity was so full that there were no com-
forters when Nineveh was overthrown. All nations
agreed with the righteousness of the activity of the
wrath of God.

When God acted thus in wrath, His action meant
complete destruction. This is poetically described by
the prophet, and it is well to repeat and to remember
that the poetic description found in Nahum has become
actual history in the course of time. We are familiar
with the historic account outside this Biblical prediction of what happened. Deodorous Seculus had prophe-
sied that Nineveh would never fall until the river became its enemy. There came a time when during an
attack the river broke its banks, and washed away the
walls for twenty stadia. Through that breach the at-

tacking forces swept in, and Nineveh was destroyed. Whereas historians on the earth level might speak of the unfortunate coincidence of the river overflowing its banks when it did, we know from this inspired account that it was the act of God. He used the river.

We inquire, then, what this message has to say to us concerning God. The first fact is that to believe in the love of God is to be quite sure of His wrath. Love can be angry under certain conditions, indeed it must be angry. It is impossible today to be complaisant in the presence of the misery, the bloodshed, the brutality, the cruelty manifested, and if we are complaisant, we may be sure that God is angry. Whenever or wherever humanity is wronged and spoiled, the anger of God is not only aroused, it becomes active. We may fittingly remind ourselves in this connection of words of our Master:

"Woe unto the world because of occasions of stumbling! for it must needs be that the occasions come; but woe to that man through whom the occasion cometh!"

The prophecy of Nahum reveals with startling clarity the sins against which the wrath of God proceeds. The first is that of pride, the lifting up of the heart in self-satisfaction, due either to the ignorance of God, or the putting Him out of account. With that God is ever angry, because of the results it produces.

Moreover, His wrath always becomes active in the presence of cruelty in any form. That anger is increased where, in spite of patience, there is still impenitence:

"He that being often reproved hardeneth his neck.
Shall suddenly be broken, and that without remedy."

With all this in mind, we return to those clear declarations of the prophet:

"The Lord is slow to anger . . . the Lord is good,
a Stronghold in the day of trouble, and He knoweth
them that put their trust in Him."

The wrath of God is ever His "strange act," but it is
necessary in the interest of His righteousness and His
love. In view of these facts we listen again to the
words of the Psalmist:

"Kiss the Son, lest He be angry, and ye perish in
the way."

VIII

THE VOICE OF ZEPHANIAH

The Severity and Goodness of God

SCRIPTURE LESSON: ZEPHANIAH 1:1-6; 3:14-20; 2 PETER 3:10-18.

"I will utterly consume all things from off the face of the ground, saith the Lord."

"The Lord thy God is in the midst of thee, a mighty One Who will save; He will rejoice over thee with joy, He will rest in His love, He will joy over thee with singing."—ZEPHANIAH 1:2; 3:17.

THE two statements are chosen because they focus attention upon a contrast which characterizes the prophecy of Zephaniah. That contrast may be described as a revelation of the severity and goodness of God. Zephaniah brings before us the terror and the tenderness of love. So marked is the contrast that some expositors have declared that the two presentations of God cannot possibly be the work of the same man, and they have, therefore, divided Zephaniah upon the basis of their own understanding of God.

Now, as a matter of fact, that union of characteristics is exactly what may be expected. The Christian Church today constantly refers to John as the apostle of love, and rightly so. It is well, therefore, to remember that Jesus surnamed him and his brother, Boanerges, sons of thunder. Those familiar with the writings of John will remember his use of two words that may almost be called key words, for they so often recur. The one is *love*, and the other is *commandments*. Throughout his writings he insists upon the value and supremacy of love, but it is equally true that no writer is more consistent in his revelations of the importance of law or commandments. Here, then, we find the same things, goodness and severity, terror and tenderness.

With all reverence we may remind ourselves of the fact that the two things are also found ultimately and superlatively in the teaching of our Lord. We should never forget that the same lips that said: "Come unto Me, all ye that labor . . . and I will rest you," also said, "Woe unto you, ye generation of vipers." Here once more we have severity and goodness, the terror and the tenderness of love.

We remember once more that all these prophetic voices were principally national in their application. It is nevertheless true how conscious the prophets were of the fact that a nation consists of the sum total of the individuals that make it up. Whereas, therefore, the application is first national, it has its personal bearing, and it is in that way that we consider it now.

The key to the book of Zephaniah is found really in the phrase "the day of the Lord," and that phrase must be interpreted necessarily by the prophet's use and application of it. We realize that this phrase is not peculiar to Zephaniah. Most of the prophets used it, or some modification of it. In our meditation on the Message of Joel we saw how he used it on five distinct occasions, and in his use showed how it represents a principle of perpetual method and application whichever moves into clearer manifestation. In other words Joel said in effect, The day of the Lord is here; the day of the Lord is imminent; the day of the Lord is postponed in finality to the ultimate. A locust plague had swept the country. He said: That is the day of the Lord. Invading armies were approaching. He declared: The day of the Lord is coming. Then, having noticed that gap in the process of history of the dispensation of the Spirit, looking on and beyond, he saw the ultimate day of the Lord.

Now Zephaniah used the phrase more frequently than any other prophet the record of whose word is preserved for us, and in the process of his argument he gives us an interpretation of its meaning.

Whenever we find it either in the Old Testament or the New, we discover that the prophet or the apostle is suggesting a contrast. The contrast is ever that of the difference between the day of man and the day of the Lord. The day of man is ever that of failure and breakdown, and these prophetic and apostolic messengers saw clearly the difference between that day and the day of the Lord.

The day of man is the day of Jehovah's patience, during which He waits while man works out his own philosophies of life. The day of the Lord is the day in which God acts in judgment against everything that has been opposed to Him and to His holy will, and to the burning passion of His eternal love.

This is man's day. We are living in the midst of it. In the full and final sense of the word, the day of the Lord is yet to be.

The permanent value of the phrase, interpreted by its use in Zephaniah, and indeed by all the prophets, may thus be stated. In God's day there will be revealed finally through processes of judgment the fact concerning Himself. In His day He will make Himself known to the nations, purifying their lives, giving to them a purer language, so that they may fitly call upon His Name, until all peoples, even the most distant, are seen coming to Him with offerings. It is when His patient waiting is over, and in order to the ultimate well-being of the race and the realization of His holy purposes of love, that the ultimate day of the Lord will dawn.

First the severity of God is clearly declared in the words:

"I will utterly consume all things from off the face of the ground, saith the Lord."

God is portrayed as surveying human life and activity, and He declares that there is a limit to that activity, that an hour, a day is coming when He will utterly consume all things.

A little later, the prophet says:

"I will search Jerusalem with candles, and I will punish the men that are settled on their lees, that say in their heart, the Lord will not do good, neither will He do evil."

In that declaration there is an unveiling of the underlying cause of all the things of evil and of sin. Man disbelieves in the activity of God in human affairs, and so declares that what the prophets have said is not so. The Lord has nothing to do with these matters. He will not do good. He does not bless men, neither will He do evil. He will not visit men with punishment for sin. Thus God is ostracized. His activity is denied even when His Being is admitted. Out of this issue all the conditions of life.

In this connection it is an arresting fact that Zephaniah exercised his ministry in the day of Josiah. The days of Josiah were days of reform unquestionably. He was greatly beloved. Moreover his purpose was to serve the Lord. He did this with all his heart. Now it is certainly significant that Zephaniah does not refer to these reforms. When we inquire the reason for this we find that when Josiah had purposed in his heart to bring about reforms he went to consult the prophetess, Huldah. She said to him in effect: Do all that is in thine heart. Thy purpose is a holy purpose. Restrain not thy hand, but there will be no permanent value in the work. A partial reform will result, but there will be no heart turning to God. Unquestionably there were reforms wrought under Josiah, but they were all on the surface. There was no heart repentance, and even then the people were saying: God will not do us good, and He will not harm us. He is passive.

When I am sometimes told that these old prophets are out of date, I am reminded of the conditions in the midst of which we are living today. Men are carrying on all kinds of activities, but are not recognizing their blessings as coming from God. It is not long ago since a man said to me quite frankly, "I don't owe anything to God. I have had to carve my own way, and I have made my own position." That statement was charac-

teristic of very much thinking that may not express itself in the actual words. Necessarily my reply to him
was a very simple one. I asked him how much during
the past thirty years he had paid in doctors' bills. He
was an American, and replied: "Not a red cent." I
looked at him and said, "And yet you have nothing to
thank God for?"

Now the severity of God will be manifested in the
fact that the day is coming when He will put an end to
all of these activities growing out of this attitude. His
judgment at last will issue in the desolation that inevitably follows upon the pathway of indifference to Himself and to His government.

The prophet shows very clearly how this indifference
to God expresses itself. Men are settled on their lees,
that is, indifference to God issues in a sense of security in human activity. A little further on the prophet
when speaking not so much to man individually,
though, of course, that is ever included, but to the
city, said:

"She obeyed not the voice, she received not correction: she trusted not in the Lord, she drew not
near to her God."

The result of all that is then definitely revealed:

"Her princes in the midst of her are roaring lions;
her judges are evening wolves; they leave nothing till
the morrow. Her prophets are light and treacherous
persons; her priests have profaned the sanctuary."

The princes and judges, prophets and priests whose
essential business was that of representing God, and so
ruling in equity, had all broken down, with calamitous

results; and the severity of God was revealed in the declaration, "I will consume all things."

The fact of God as a God of wrath against sin is not being apprehended or declared today to any great extent. Men are saying God will not do evil, He will not harm us. If I could be persuaded that that was true, I should refuse to believe in the goodness of God. That He could possibly be complaisant or inactive in the presence of human sin and failure is unthinkable. Peter referred to "the longsuffering of God," and the phrase is one of radiant revelation of the Divine patience. But let it not be forgotten that after the period came the Flood. If I could be persuaded that there was no judgment, no punishment, no swift and terrible retribution falling ultimately upon those who have forgotten God, and refused to obey His voice, then I should see nothing ahead but chaos.

But that is not all of the prophecy. It declares one side of truth, and it is a side closely connected with the other. We pass for a moment then to the second of the passages quoted at the beginning. It was a word spoken to a people who had heard the voice, who had repented of their ways, who had turned to God, a remnant who had refused to do iniquity, or speak lies, who were no longer using a deceitful tongue. The attitude of God to such is declared in the words:

"The Lord thy God is in the midst of thee, a mighty One Who will save; He will rejoice over thee with joy, He will rest in His love, He will joy over thee with singing."

Thus Zephaniah the prophet of the terror of the Lord,

the prophet of the severity of a holy God shows the heart of God. In doing this he begins by insisting upon His enthronement. The Lord in the midst of thee is mighty, He will save. He is mighty. That speaks of His ability. He will save. That declares His determination. He can, He will. When men return to Him as the enthroned God, they return to His power. He is able, He can. Was it not Carlyle who, in his *Heroes and Hero Worship,* said that in the last analysis the King is the man who can. This ability of power can only ultimately be postulated of God Himself. He is mighty, and the direction of the output of His might will be according to His own will and purpose.

What that activity is, is revealed in the declaration: "He will save." He will save from the calamities that follow iniquity, and infinitely more, save from that iniquity which causes the calamity.

Then follows a picture of exquisite beauty. Let me say at once it is the picture of motherhood. It suggests the mother with the child in her arms. I cannot help feeling that Zephaniah had watched such a scene. He had seen her looking at the child, and rejoicing over it. Then he had seen her so full of joy that no word escaped her. She was silent in her love. Until, finally, no longer able to remain silent, she broke forth into singing. That is the prophet's picture of God. He is mighty, He will save; and when He has done it, like a mother, He will bear us in His arms, rejoicing in His love, until He Himself is portrayed as breaking forth into song. This is the goodness of God, the tenderness of love.

The result of all this is that there comes to those who are thus saved through His might, and loved with His everlasting love, songs instead of sorrow, service instead of selfishness, solidarity instead of the scattered forces of being. In this twofold side of the Divine nature lies the safety of humanity and of the universe. If God were other than He is, as revealed in this prophecy, there would be very little hope for humanity.

"We rejoice in hope of the glory of God," because we believe in His severity, and know His goodness.

In view of this, Peter's words carry a message of vital importance. We are to give diligence that we abide in holy living and godliness, that all the actions of our life shall tend to the hastening of the coming of the Day. And, finally, lest we be seduced from our faith, we listen to the positive appeal: "Grow in the grace . . . of our Lord and Saviour Jesus Christ."

IX

THE VOICE OF HABAKKUK

The Problems of Faith

SCRIPTURE LESSON: HABAKKUK 1:1-6; 2:1-4; 3:1, 2, 16-19.

> *"For though the fig tree shall not blossom,*
> *Neither shall fruit be in the vines;*
> *The labor of the olive shall fail,*
> *And the fields shall yield no meat;*
> *The flock shall be cut off from the fold,*
> *And there shall be no herd in the stalls;*
> *Yet I will rejoice in the Lord,*
> *I will joy in the God of my salvation."*
>
> —HABAKKUK 3:17, 18.

EVERY ONE will agree that these are arresting words. There is a rhythm in their movement, and vividness in their description. That which is most impressive is the almost startling contrasts between the conditions described and the experience claimed. Notice the conditions again: the fig tree not blossoming; no fruit in the vines; the labor spent upon the olive failing; the fields barren, yielding no meat; the flock cut off from the fold; no herd in the stalls. That is the background. In the foreground we have a singer who says "Yet," notwithstanding all these things,

"I will rejoice in the Lord,

I will joy in the God of my salvation."

The picture of conditions is one of the dreariest man ever drew. It is one of the most melancholy poems ever

90

written. Nevertheless the singer is radiant and exulting, and we find that the dirge is a prelude to a pæan.

As we read, we ask ourselves: Was this man a fanatic? Was he deluded? or did he speak a wisdom of which the world knows nothing? We affirm at once our conviction that this is a song of the highest wisdom, and the singer a philosopher in possession of the true secrets of life.

Let us consider first the process which resulted in the song; secondly, inquire the ground of his confidence; and finally, examine the joy of his experience.

The whole value of this prophecy of Habakkuk on the side of human experience is its revelation of the process that led to this song. Habakkuk did not begin on this triumphant note. Addressing himself to God, he said:

"O Lord, how long shall I cry, and Thou wilt not hear? I cry unto Thee of violence, and Thou wilt not save. Why dost Thou shew me iniquity, and look upon perverseness? for spoiling and violence are before me; and there is strife, and contention riseth up. Therefore the law is slacked, and judgment doth never go forth."

That is how he began, but he ended:

"I will rejoice in the Lord,
   I will joy in the God of my salvation."

The writing of Habakkuk is peculiar in that it is not the record of an address or addresses, delivered to his people. It is strictly a narrative. In that matter it is like the book of Jonah. That also was a narrative written by Jonah, recording his own experiences. Here once more we have a book in which the writer is telling his own story.

After these opening inquiries, revealing depression, we follow the process until we reach the song. There are three things noticeable, the first being that he reached a song of confidence through a doubt which was perfectly honest. Next he reached the song through trials in the midst of which he waited upon his watch-tower. Finally, he reached the song because, as the result of his statement of honest doubt, and of his waiting and watching, he received from God a declaration revealing the deepest secrets of life.

First then, he was in doubt, and was perfectly honest about it. He was living in the midst of terrible anarchy. The sentences already read reveal this quite clearly. To express the attitude of his mind very bluntly, and perhaps in language with which we are familiar today, God was doing nothing, so it appeared to Habakkuk. Violence abounded, cruelty was rampant, crime was flagrant, lust was everywhere, and God seemed inactive.

That was the burden of his inquiry: "O Lord, how long?" In the "How long?" there is the revelation of an underlying faith, while yet there is an equally clear revelation of an imminent doubt. Why was it that God did not do something in the midst of these appalling conditions? We can readily understand the attitude of mind, and men of faith have often been driven to ask such questions. The very hour in which we are now living is one in which very many are conscious of the same sense of difficulty.

What is arresting is that when Habakkuk asked the question, he asked it of God. It is quite possible under such circumstances to form a Society to discuss the matter. To do this is still to remain in the darkness. This man spoke of the matter to God. Thus through doubt honestly faced, through an agony of mind from which, for the moment, he found no escape, he spoke to God.

In answer to this honest speech of Habakkuk, God declared in effect that although His servant did not discern the Divine activity, He nevertheless was acting. God declared to him not only that He was doing something, but He was doing that which if He told Habakkuk, he would not believe Him. To me there was a touch of tender humor in the very answer that God thus first made to him. Having said this, He continued, and did declare what it was that He was doing. He showed that while Habakkuk was troubled by the violence in the midst of which he was living, and troubled by the consciousness of an impending invading force, that this very threatened invasion on the part of the Chaldeans was under the government of God. The activity of His government was proceeding outside His own people, in order to deal with them.

Then, to adopt the language of simplicity, Habakkuk said in his heart: But this is worse than ever. This is utterly beyond my understanding. I cannot see how God can use the Chaldeans. I cannot understand how God, going outside the regular channels of His operations, can use such a people, characterized by pride and cruelty.

Then came the great moment in the life of Habakkuk, when he said: I will get me to the watchtower. I
will wait and see what it all means. That was the second phase in the process. He saw the approaching foe.
He had heard that he was approaching under the Divine government. It was when he thus waited on the
watchtower that God gave him the secret of life in
those remarkable words that we are apt to quote not
always in their fulness. God said to him:

"Behold, his soul is puffed up, it is not upright in
him; but the just shall live by his faith."

Here is a contrast. With reverence we may attempt to
interpret. It is as though God said: Your opinion of
the Chaldeans is correct. The nation is "puffed up."
That is one way and attitude of life. The contrasting
attitude is, "The just shall live by his faith." "Just"
is undoubtedly the true translation, though necessarily
faith is included. The declaration then is that it is by
faith that the just live.

Nothing is here said of the issue of the puffed up and
crooked. The inevitable issue is, however, that they
perish. On the other hand the just live. Thus in the
declaration Habakkuk was brought face to face with
the contrast between the way of life which inevitably
ends in destruction, and the way of life which inevitably is that of continuity.

It was after this that Habakkuk sang his song. It
is interesting to observe that the Psalm is headed:

"A prayer of Habakkuk the prophet, set to Shigionoth."

Dr. Thirtle, in his remarkably illuminative volume on

the Psalms and their captions, said that the word Shigionoth simply means *loud cries*. It is found prefacing one other Psalm only in the Bible collection, namely, Psalm seven. It is intended to give character to the poem and the music. The song, therefore, consists of loud cries, and we must ever interpret the nature of these cries by the surrounding context. In Psalm seven they were the cries of a man in his agony. Here they were the cries of a man exulting in joy.

Thus if we ask upon what grounds this man could base such a song, we have found the answer to our inquiries. First, he was honest about his doubting. Then he waited on his watchtower. Then he listened for the voice of God, and hearing it, received the true interpretation of life. It was confidence in this that turned his dirge into a pæan of praise.

The confirmation of the Divine statement is found in all history, and especially we may say in this case, in the history of the people of God to which people Habakkuk belonged. Reviewing that history it was possible for him to realize that if everything were destroyed, God was able to create. It may be well that we remind ourselves at this point that if we grant the first miracle, "In the beginning God created," everything is possible. It is what Habakkuk came to realize anew. Moreover, by the activity of this God, chaos becomes cosmos. The present might be that of a wilderness and desert, but when God is recognized it becomes certain that,

"The wilderness and the solitary place shall be

glad; and the desert shall rejoice, and blossom as the rose."

He knew from that same history, moreover, that God is able to send supplies from sources of which we know nothing. Israel had left Egypt and found herself in the wilderness, and there all their need had been supplied, manna and quails and water.

And yet again he knew from the history of his own people that God is able to multiply the little, so that it becomes the much. That was the experience of the wilderness, and individually it was the experience of a woman in the story of the prophet. The barrel of meal and the cruse of oil grew no less.

And yet further, this history taught him that God is able to sustain without food; Moses in the mount for forty days; Elijah in Horeb for forty days. When fig tree and vine and olive fail, fields are barren, flocks and herds are dying, there will be nothing left. Oh, yes, there will be—there will be God.

Yet was there not something deeper than all that? Supposing God creates no new thing, sends no supply from hidden sources, does not multiply the little, does not sustain without food, and we weaken and die— what then? Even then we rejoice in the Lord, because He will not withdraw Himself; and in Him there is a fulness complete, and joy preëminently satisfying, a peace undisturbed. The Psalm of Habakkuk harmonizes with the great cry of Job:

"Though He slay me, yet will I wait for Him."

In conclusion, let us examine the joy of Habakkuk's experience. To translate literally from the Hebrew would almost startle us. To do that is to find that he said: "I will jump for joy in the Lord; I will spin round, so filled with gladness that he speaks so hilarious, so filled with gladness that he speaks of dancing and spinning round. His joy was exuberant, and could only find expression in such language. Notice, however, that it was in "Jehovah," in the "God of salvation," that he had such an experience. It was not the result of circumstances, but of triumph over them.

The process, then, that led to the joy was first of all the knowledge of God which inspired him to declare his doubt in His presence. It came, therefore, from the correction of his doubt in fellowship with God.

The value of this story for us is self-evident. We are living in a day when we are very much inclined to say, "How long?" Peter in one of his letters declared: "We have the word of prophecy made more sure." The ratification of everything in these great prophetic messages is to be found in Christ. That is why Paul wrote: "Rejoice in the Lord alway," and unless someone should not have caught the idea, or have felt the impact of the injunction, he said: "And again I say, Rejoice." All the things concerning God found their fulfilment in Christ. He acted in the realm of creation. He was able to supply from hidden resources, and to multiply the little into the much, as when He broke the five loaves.

Consequently it is for us ever to rejoice in Him. Prevailing conditions are appalling. We find ourselves in the midst of violence and cruelty and oppression and evil. We are inclined to think that God is inactive. If we are quiet and listen to Him, He is saying to us what He did to Habakkuk, that He was acting even though we cannot see or understand. He it is Who is girding and governing oftentimes those outside the covenant, but always that their coöperation may be compelled in His march toward the ultimate realization of His purpose.

It is true today that those who are lifted up, whose souls are crooked, are doomed. It is true that those who have faith, live and abide.

Our joy is always in proportion to our confidence in God, and our confidence in God is in proportion to our knowledge of Him. It is out of such knowledge and such confidence that the song will proceed, and with Cowper we may join in the song that repeats for our days the song of Habakkuk:

> "Sometimes a light surprises
>   The Christian while he sings;
> It is the Lord Who rises
>   With healing in His wings.
> When comforts are declining,
>   He grants the soul, again,
> A season of clear shining,
>   To cheer it after rain.
>
> .   .   .   .   .
>
> "Though vine nor fig-tree neither
>   Their wonted fruit shall bear;
> Though all the fields should wither,
>   Nor flocks nor herds be there;
> Yet, God the same abiding,
>   His praise shall tune my voice;
> For while in Him confiding,
>   I cannot but rejoice."

X

THE VOICE OF HAGGAI

Relative Values

SCRIPTURE LESSON: HAGGAI 1.

"Is it a time for you yourselves to dwell in your ceiled houses, while this house lieth waste?"—HAGGAI 1:4.

IN these words the prophet Haggai rebuked the people of his time for a failure which resulted from a loss, on their part, of the true sense of relative values.

The Temple lay in ruins, or rather in an unfinished condition, in which it had continued for fifteen years. When they had returned from captivity they began to build, but when threatened by their enemies they ceased. The years had passed and nothing stood but perhaps the first courses upon the foundations. It goes without saying that by this time the work was overgrown with grass and silted with rubbish.

The word of the Lord now came to His people through Haggai, demanding that they should arise and build the House. The question asked was really an answer to the statement which the people were making in order to excuse themselves from building the Temple. Their duty was to build. They knew it, and had known it long; but they were saying:

"It is not the time for us to come, the time for the
Lord's House to be built."

It is quite easy for us to understand the attitude, for it
has often recurred. People are very fond of declaring
that things ought to be done, but the time has not yet
come. To adopt modern phraseology, the people declared that the psychic moment had not arrived, even
when the spiritual opportunity was waiting.

It was to that statement, then, that the question of
the text was the answer. In it there is a contrast, indeed a threefold contrast, a contrast of persons, a contrast of houses, and a contrast of conditions.

In the contrast of persons, One is not named, and
that is God, Whose House lay in ruins. But the people are named, and named indeed in a remarkable way.
"Is it a time for you yourselves?" This is an occasion
when, not quarreling with the translation, I nevertheless feel that something might have been gained if the
Hebrew had been more bluntly rendered. We should
then have a repetition of the word "you," unquestionably with an emphasis on the second occurrence.

"Is it a time for you, *you* to dwell in your ceiled
houses?"

That repetition of the "you" shows that he was reminding these people of whom they really were. They were
a people with a remarkable history, with a definite
knowledge of God, with a clear conception of the supreme importance of the Temple of God.

The contrast is next between houses, "your houses,"
"this House." The reference was to the places in
which they dwelt, to which they retired for quietness

and rest, where their home life was found, "your houses." God's House was the place appointed for His meeting with His people in fellowship.

Then we have the contrast of conditions. They were dwelling in "ceiled houses," which means houses embellished with beauty in every way, costly houses, expensive houses. The people had been remarkably prosperous during the fifteen years, and they had built for themselves "ceiled houses." In contrast, "this House" lay waste, incomplete, overgrown with weeds.

They said it was not the time to build. They believed in the importance of building, but they were waiting for what they thought of as a more opportune moment.

The evil revealed is common, is destructive, is insidious. These people were thoroughly orthodox, but just then the supreme things were relegated to a subsidiary position. Materially they had been successful. They had built their own ceiled houses, but at the moment trouble was threatening, and so it seemed quite reasonable to declare that the time had not come for building the Temple.

In the first movement of the prophecy, Haggai had suggested to them a way of correction. Twice over he called them to consider; first to consider their ways, and see how things had failed. They had sown much and brought in little. They ate, and had not enough. They drank, but were not filled. They were clothed, but were not warm. They had been putting money away, but into a bag with holes. There was a fine scorn in this description, and in all likelihood it was intended to describe a spiritual rather than an actual material condition.

Again calling them to consider their ways, they were charged to go to the mountain, and cut wood, and build the House of God.

Such is the ancient story, and the revelation it brings to us is that of the importance of relative values, the importance of putting first things first, and the consequent disaster of looking upon that which is supreme as though it were secondary.

In the light of the question, let us attempt to look at our modern conditions. Let us consider the disaster which results from this failure, and that in order that we may also consider how the failure may be corrected.

The applications can be made in national, social, and individual life. We forget relative values in national life when we put revenue before righteousness; when we consider personality as being less important than property; when we put man before God. Of all these things illustrations might be adduced in the life of our nation today. If we study the statute books of the nation we shall find that there are more laws on those books in defense of property than in defense of children. If we read the news of the Police Courts we often find sentences passed which reveal the fact that punishment is heavier upon those who do wrong to possessions and property than those who do wrong to human personality. I realize that in the last period of our history there has been a vast improvement in these matters, but we are not yet by any means clear.

Without dwelling upon particular illustrations, let it be said that when man's desire is considered before God's law, and when we propose to lower that law to meet the desires of men and women, we are failing to put first things first. Such action ever grows out of, and then accentuates, a lowered conception of man. No man really thinks highly of a man except the one who sees him in the image and likeness of God, and understands that his well-being must be found within the will of God.

Or passing from these wider matters, if we consider our social life, that is, the inter-relationship between man and man, we are failing to put first things first when we make a bread basis the reason for social activities, instead of such being the result of a spiritual conception. We are ever confusing values when we put conditions of life before character. We thank God for every activity which characterizes our times for the clearing out of the slums, but we need to remember that if we are more anxious about tenements than tenants, we are failing.

In the realm of art the same truth applies. That the people should have art presented to them I agree, but when we put expression in art before spiritual capacity to discern it, we shall only produce an art that blasts rather than blesses.

The whole trouble with us is that we are more concerned with things than with life. And yet this age is almost mastered by a passion for things, and very often things are supposed to be valuable in proportion as they do not belong to the other man. There is a self-centered passion to possess which is a peril to the whole social fabric.

When we come to the individual application we see at once that when a man is more concerned with a living than with life, when his thoughts in the morning and his activity through the day are centered upon the support of that which is transient, to the neglect of the permanent, he is failing to put first things first. So when we put recreation before creation, when amusement is sought as a stimulant or as a narcotic, when man is more anxious to be filled with wine wherein is riot than with the Holy Spirit of God, he is certainly not putting first things first. When we place possession before principle, and our goods are everything, and God's rights are nothing, we are disastrously failing.

The result of all such attitudes in national life are disastrous. The nation passes under bondage to sin, enters into the toils of baseness, puts its neck under the yoke of wrong, and that means the decadence of its manhood. Such paralysis of national life must result in disaster, no counsel sufficiently wise to guide, and no strength equal to the demands made upon life. We have largely forgotten God, and put Him out of count, even though every now and then, on some great occasion, we make a gesture in His direction. We may gather round the sacred shrine of the Cenotaph and sing:

"O God our Help in ages past,
    Our Hope for years to come,
Our Shelter from the stormy blast,
    And our eternal home."

and as we sing, remain hypocrites, not believing really
that our hope for years to come is in Him.

In social life, when first things are not put first, the
result is animalism, and men and women say, even
though they may not use the actual words:

"Let us eat and drink, for tomorrow we die."
Sometimes it is said with a groan, and yet with a careless chuckle, forgetting that it is the expression of vi-
cious animalism. Whenever these things are so, the
national life is on its way to destruction, in spite of all
attempts to improve what we speak of as conditions.
If we take a man who has been living in a slum area,
and put him to live in a garden city, and his character
is not right, he will turn the garden into a slum.

Moreover, such attitudes and actions will create an
incapacity for the very things possessed. It is possible
for a man to own something, and yet never possess it.
Blind people may own pictures, and never see them.
Deaf men may listen to the strains of the "Messiah"
without hearing them. Men and women may be in the
presence of the flower in the crannied wall, and even
pluck it out of the crannies and hold it in their hand,
and yet never see God. A man may own broad acres
and yet never possess them because his own life is mastered by false conceptions of relative values.

The application to the individual soul is that such
failure to discern and apply first things issues in spiritual death, and consequently in moral decline. To the
individual the rebound from stimulant is deadly inertia.
There is a death from which there can be no resurrec-
tion. Men say, "My goods, my goods, my goods," and

a voice in the night speaks with the infinite satire of eternity:

"This night is thy soul required of thee; and the things which thou hast prepared, whose shall they be?"

All the figures of speech of the prophet in his first movement apply. Toil without recompense is poverty. Eating without feeding is hunger. Drink without quenching is undying thirst. Clothing without warmth is the chilly fact of death. Wages without purchasing power is disillusionment, the husks without the kernel, the frame without the picture, life without living.

What is the cure? The answer is simply that it is found in the restored sense of relative values. God and His House must be first; His glory, His grace, His claim.

Then as to ourselves and our surroundings. There must be a new recognition of our dependence and of our duty. Supremely the cure is to be found in restored personal relationship with God. Without God nothing is good. Quarles, quaint as he certainly was, was right when he said:

"Without Thy presence, earth gives no refection;
    Without Thy presence, sea affords no treasure;
Without Thy presence, air's a rank infection;
    Without Thy presence, heaven's itself no pleasure.
If not possessed, if not enjoyed in Thee,
    What's earth, or sea, or air, or heaven to me?

"In having all things, and not Thee, what have I?
    Not having Thee, what have my labors got?
Let me enjoy but Thee, what further crave I?
    And having Thee alone, what have I not?

I wish not sea nor land; nor would I be
Possessed of heaven, heaven unpossessed of Thee!"

There is nothing more important than that we should awake, in our national life, to the realization of the fact that righteousness is revenue, that personality is property. In our social life we must again understand that when the Kingdom of God is sought, all things are added which are necessary; and in individual life there must be a return to the realization of the fact that it is life that matters, and that in its relationship with the supreme things. Thus we may say nothing is more important than a true sense of proportion. Nationally, God first; socially, man before the conditions in which he lives; individually, the soul before the body.

It would be well for us to remember the words of the singer of Israel as he said:

"Surely I will not come into the tabernacle of my house,

Nor go up into my bed;

I will not give sleep to mine eyes,

Or slumber to mine eyelids;

Until I find out a place for the Lord,

A tabernacle for the Mighty One of Jacob."

When we take up that attitude, we may hear the voice of God speaking through the prophet Isaiah:

"For thus saith the high and lofty One that inhabiteth eternity, Whose Name is Holy: I dwell in the high and holy place, with him also that is of a contrite and humble spirit, to revive the spirit of the humble, and to revive the heart of the contrite ones."

XI

THE VOICE OF ZECHARIAH

The Coming Age

SCRIPTURE LESSON: ZECHARIAH 8:1-17.

"And the streets of the city shall be full of boys and girls, playing in the streets thereof."—ZECHARIAH 8:5.

ZECHARIAH was contemporary with Haggai. A careful reading of the two prophets will show that the earlier messages of Zechariah are dated, as those of Haggai are. In these earlier movements they alternated in the delivery of their messages, and all were aimed at compelling the nation to build the Temple of God.

Zechariah, however, went beyond Haggai, and he has been aptly called the apocalyptic writer of the Old Testament. In a series of symbolic visions he watched the process of things through the ages, and in the chapter from which our text is taken we reach the point where he saw, beyond all the desolation, restoration; beyond the punitive judgments of God, His return to His people on account of their repentance, and the establishment of the new Divine order.

Ever and anon these old Hebrew seers from some high point of vision caught glimpses of the coming glory, a glory which has not yet come, but which undoubtedly is coming. They heard, moreover, some notes of the final harmony. These men saw the city of God afar off. They saw the walls of that city. They saw the conditions obtaining when the city is built, and the Kingdom of God is established.

Among such visions there is none in my judgment more graphic or full of suggestiveness than that contained in the words of our text. Looking on, Zechariah saw a city, and it was a city of an earthly order, for he saw old men and women there, leaning upon their staff for very age; but he also saw that:

"The streets of the city shall be full of boys and girls, playing in the streets thereof."

I was born and brought up in a period when a text like that would be looked upon with some amount of questionings. I remember how a boy of my own age, an acquaintance, who found Christ, in the exuberance of his joy after joining the Church, putting his hands on the tea table, where it was spread, and vaulting clean over it. His mother said in a sharp voice, "George, you have joined the Church." This is a simple but revealing incident. The dear woman did not think that a boy who had joined the Church could do anything so revealing of exuberance of spirit. The period to which I refer has, to a large extent, passed; and yet its attitudes are still found in the minds of some men and women. One can almost hear most excellent people, as the text is announced, saying: Should not that be praying, instead of playing? No, the prophet did not say praying, but playing. Moreover, he saw them playing in the streets, and that seems more appalling. The final thing, however, is that there were boys and girls evidently playing together.

Now if it should be that there are any who think the declaration is a strange one, it is quite evident that the prophet himself knew there would be people surprised at it, for in the very next sentence he says:

"If it be marvelous in the eyes of the remnant of this people in those days, should it also be marvelous in Mine eyes? saith the Lord of hosts."

In other words, God declared that what might surprise His people did not surprise Him. That boys and girls should be able to play together in the streets reveals the goal of the Divine purpose. Today, if I really want a glimpse of the city of God that is to be, I shall not attend a Sunday service to see it, but rather go to a park on a Saturday afternoon, or to some place where children play. I shall go rather to a playground than to a prayer meeting.

No one will imagine that I am undervaluing the Sunday service or the prayer meeting, but in these things we do not see the Kingdom of God as it is going to be, as clearly as when we watch the groups of children playing together. There are discrepancies in both I doubt not, but in that playground filled with playing children I am nearer understanding the Divine ideal than if I am studying politics, or commerce, or law.

It is interesting to find how old commentators found in this text a revelation of security for the adult population. I found one who said the text teaches the multiplication of children, and reveals the times as peaceful times. That may be good, but it shuts out the child interest. From that standpoint let us consider it.

And the first thing we observe is that the text affords a revelation of God's purpose for the child; and then that it shows clearly the close relationship between the attitude and condition of children, and the condition of the city and of the nation.

The thought is perfectly patent that the thought of God for children is that they should play. Other Kingdom references to the ultimate victory in the old prophets describe children playing.

"The sucking child shall play on the hole of the asp, the weaned child on the cockatrice den . . . the wolf shall dwell with the lamb, and the leopard shall lie down with the kid; and the calf and the young lion and the fatling together; and a little child shall lead them."

Thus the child is seen playing near to Nature. I expect that any one who has taken a child to the Zoological Gardens has found it a little difficult to explain to the child that it is not safe for it to climb over the rails and get near to the animals. And yet that is just what the child wants to do. It is the natural and proper instinct of its life.

We pause for a moment with the thought suggested by the word "playing." Ruskin said:

"Play is an exertion of the body or mind made to please ourselves."

That is true up to a certain point. Many a youth, controlling a motor for business purposes, looks upon it as drudgery. The same youth, driving a motor of his own, looks upon it as pleasure. It is important to remember that play always means work. If we have any doubt, we may take a day off from our business and stay, let us say, with a four year old boy or girl, doing all they do from morning to night. I think we shall be convinced that play involves work. Play does, however, mean preparation for work. If child life be rightly understood, it will yield up the revelation of the underlying capacity of the child, and it will play its way into work.

Perhaps with some apology I may illustrate in my own life's story. I played my way into preaching, for I preached when I was six, seven, eight, to my sister's dolls. It was a great game, and I have been at it ever since, and that statement does not mean that it is trifling. It has been strenuous work, sometimes characterized by agony and soul travail; but it has always been playtime.

Another thing arresting is that boys and girls were seen by the prophet playing together. For a long time now in our educational system and in our Youth Associations we have been careful to keep them apart. It is interesting to be reminded that our families are made up of boys and girls, and in the fellowship of the family the strength of the boy serves the girl, and the refinement of the girl saves the boy from roughness. I am not proposing to deal with this at any length, but refer to it.

Tarrying for a moment with the declaration that play is a preparation for work, we may observe also that the child will play at things which its elders are doing seri-

ously. A somewhat sad illustration is the presence of
toy soldiers, and toy cannons, and toy airplanes in our
stores. In the city of God children will not play at
war, neither will they play at kings and slaves. I think
perhaps in the earliest period after the establishment
of the Kingdom, they may play at blacksmith's shop,
beating swords into ploughshares and spears into prun-
ing hooks. The one certain thing is that they play as
they watch their elders.

We now turn to consider what this means as to public life in the coming Kingdom. The prophet saw that
Kingdom centralized in a metropolis, in a city, and the
fact that children were playing in the streets of it shows
how then the child will be the test of public life.

This may be put very simply and briefly by two
statements. First, if in the city of God the streets are
to be full of boys and girls playing, it is evident that the
streets will be fit for boys and girls to play in; and,
secondly, that boys and girls will be fit to play in the
streets.

Thus, in the suggested declaration we have an indi-
cation of the order of life in the city as to its authority
and its activities. Moreover, the light of the statement
flashes through doors, and into the homes, for out of
those houses, through those doors the children come.

First, then, the streets are such as the children may
play in. That means, to quote another prophet:

"They shall not hurt nor destroy in all My holy
    mountain."

The streets will be fit for the children physically, mentally, and spiritually. In the city of God there will

be nothing left unattended to, which being neglected would put the child in any physical peril. Drainage? Certainly. Traffic? Absolutely. In the city of God the safety of the child will be the first care, and when we have secured that, we shall have secured the safety of all the citizens.

Mentally, too, there will be nothing to harm the child. No impure literature will be on sale. No evil placards, intended to suggest, and no unholy pictures exhibited before the eyes of the child. The love of the child will be higher than the love of gain in the city of God.

Finally, the spiritual interest of the child will be supreme. Christ's word will be absolutely realized that rather than cause a little one to stumble, it were better that a millstone be hanged about the neck, and that the one causing the offence should be drowned in the depths of the sea. The salvation of the child is the salvation of society.

Moreover, it is equally true that home life will be what it ought to be, so that the children passing into the streets carry with them no polluting influences.

The question naturally arises as to how these things will be brought about. There is only one answer. This is the Kingdom of God, and the Kingdom of God vested in the authority of the Christ of God. When Christ is King, when all the authorities in the city are under His guidance and administration, then these things will follow as naturally as the dawning of the morning breaks forth after the darkness of the night. When our streets are ready for the play of the children, then the city of God will have arrived.

The proportion in which children are safe today is the measure of the working of the Spirit of Christ in our own age, and thank God there has been a wonderful growth in that direction during the last half century. As I go about London I am impressed with what happens when school-time is over. Near the exit from the school a policeman stands, and one of the most beautiful things I know is to see that policeman with two or three bairns clinging to him, laughing up into his face until he leads them across the road.

All this necessitates the inquiry as to what we have done to make our city safe for the children. It is sometimes said that these matters municipal are outside the realm of Christian thought and activity. That is not true. Here we have, unless we are renegade, to bring to bear the teaching and ideals of Christ, as well as to make known His Gospel of redemption.

Necessarily again it is important that we should realize what this means as to home life. There are children who would pollute the streets by their very presence, and that applies to suburbs as well as to slums. Where this is so, blame does not attach to the children, but to the homes from which they come. In the Kingdom of God the words some of you have hanging in your homes will be a living reality:

> "Christ is the Head of this house,
> The unseen Guest at every meal,
> The Silent Listener to every conversation."

Where that is true, children will pass out to play, kind, unselfish, pure. The conditions for the highest and best playfulness of children are created in the home where obedience is won rather than enforced, where trust is inspired and never given reason for breakdown, where high ideals are presented, where the conversation of adults concerning others is never hard or unkind in the listening ears of childhood. Homes are the strength of nations. The family is still God's first circle of society, upon which all others are to be based in nature and government.

When we contrast that picture with much which we see, first, we thank God for everything that moves in its direction, and yet how much there is to sadden. We think of multitudes of children, not our own, living in a polluted atmosphere, amid wealth, or amid the deep depression of poverty; and we realize how much there is to be done.

We always thank God for one man who now has passed over, Benjamin Waugh, and the wonderful work he did for children.

Perhaps it will be helpful to recall Mrs. Barratt Browning's lines:

"The young lambs are bleating in the meadow;
    The young birds are chirping in the nest;
The young fawns are playing in the shadows,
    The young flowers are blooming towards the west—
But the young, young children, O my brothers,
    They are weeping bitterly—
They are weeping in the playtime of the others,
    In the country of the free.

"Do you hear the children weeping and disproving,
    O my brothers, what ye preach?
For God's possible is taught by His world's loving,
    And the children doubt of each.

And well may the children weep before you;
    They are weary as they run;
But the child's sob curseth deeper in the silence,
    Than the strong man in his wrath."

Our business then is first and last to set up the reign
of Christ in our own hearts and in our own homes.
Then we may turn our attention to civic affairs, and aim
for evermore to make the streets fit for the children.

"Come to me, O ye children,
    For I hear you at your play.
And the questions that perplexed me
    Have vanished quite away.

"Ye open the eastern windows
    That look toward the sun,
Where thoughts are singing swallows,
    And the brooks of morning run.

"Ye are better than all the ballads
    That ever were sung or said;
For ye are living poems,
    And all the rest are dead."

XII

THE VOICE OF MALACHI

The Last Message

SCRIPTURE LESSON: MALACHI 3:13—4:6.

"I have loved you, saith the Lord. Yet ye say, Wherein hast Thou loved us?"—MALACHI 1:2a.

I DO not hesitate to say that there are senses in which no more startling verse than this is found in all the Bible. It is the record of God and man speaking to each other. God declares: "I have loved you," and the answer of the man in effect is, I do not see it, "Wherein hast Thou loved us?"

Such a verse demands careful attention, and we inquire under what circumstances this conversation took place. It is almost universally admitted that Malachi was the last of the Old Testament prophets in historic sequence, and there can be no doubt that his messages were closely associated with the work of Nehemiah. Indeed, before studying Malachi it is good to study the book of Nehemiah, for there we find the historic background. Whereas it is true that Malachi is not mentioned either in the book of Ezra or Nehemiah, it is quite evident that if he was not contemporary with them, he certainly followed their work very closely. If we compare the closing part of Nehemiah with this prophecy, we shall see the failures of the people that angered Nehemiah, inspired the message of Malachi. The book of Nehemiah has a fascination all its own, as it presents to us a very remarkable man. When we consider the conditions under which he worked, we find that the priesthood was defiled, foreign marriages were cursing the people, and the payment of the tithe was neglected. Now these are the very things with which Malachi dealt.

The spirit of the people is revealed in Malachi very clearly, and in a somewhat curious way. What I mean will be found as I read seven sentences scattered across the book.

The first is in our text: "Wherein hast Thou loved us?" The second is found in the sixth verse of the same chapter: "Wherein have we despised Thy Name?" The next follows in the next verse: "Wherein have we polluted Thee?" In chapter two, in verse seventeen, we find: "Wherein have we wearied Thee?" In chapter three, verse seven: "Wherein shall we return?" In verse eight: "Wherein have we robbed Thee?" and in verse thirteen: "Wherein have we spoken against Thee?" That word "Wherein" really is the key to the book, and is a startling revelation of the attitude of the people. To every charge brought against them they replied by using the word. In other words, Malachi was speaking to people who protested against the charges he was making.

The whole prophecy reveals a calloused people and a sensitive God. It is well to remember that it was to Israel he spoke, and when he used the word he was not referring merely to the Northern kingdom, nor to the

Southern kingdom of Judah, but to the whole nation. In this connection it is well to remember that when, after the captivity, these people returned, only a remnant of them came back, first under Ezra, and then another contingent later on; but those who did return consisted not only of the tribe of Judah, but members of all the tribes, so that the message was delivered to the whole nation. Undoubtedly the larger number of them were of Judah, but members of the other tribes were included.

As in the book of Nehemiah we have the last fragment of inspired Hebrew history; so in the prophecy of Malachi, we have the last fragment of inspired Hebrew prophecy. There was no other authentic prophet until the coming of John the Baptist. During the Maccabean period remarkable men were raised up, but of that period we have no inspired history, and there arose no authentic prophet.

If we go back a hundred years in the history of the people we find that Haggai and Zachariah had brought them back to the point of responsibility for the rebuilding of the Temple. As the result of their ministry everything was restored. The city was built, the walls surrounded it, the Temple was there, the priests were in their places, the sacrifices were being offered. Then Malachi came, and brought the burden, or the oracle of the Word of the Lord to Israel, and the opening sentence is, "I have loved you," and the answer is recorded, "Wherein hast Thou loved us?"

Taking the book as a whole then, we discover three matters which constitute a living message to our own

times. The first is that we have revealed the unfailing
love of Jehovah; the second that we see the appalling
failure of human life in the presence of that unfailing
love; and finally we have an unveiling of the secrets of
strength of those who really know God in the midst
of such failure.

The unfailing love of God is declared in these opening words: "I have loved you, saith the Lord." Beautiful as that translation is, I feel that it misses something of the essential thought and meaning of the Hebrew. I am not suggesting that it is inaccurate, but
that it is incomplete. The Hebrew language is infinitely richer in its tenses than our English, and the
tense here employed suggests something far more than
"I have loved you," which is a past tense. The Hebrew
tense marks continuity. It does not look back only,
but around and on, and I think may be rendered for
our more accurate apprehension, I have loved, I do
love, I will love you, saith the Lord.

With this background of the last page of inspired
history for four hundred years, and the last page of
inspired prophecy for the like period, we have this great
declaration of the persistence of the love of God. It
was Shakespeare who said:

> "Love is not love,
> That alters when it alteration finds."

A wonderful statement, but if true, then we do not
know much about love on the human level. But that is
God's love, love that does not alter when it alteration
finds.

If we glance over the prophecy again, noting the occasions upon which the question "Wherein" occurs, we shall find in every case it was asked in answer to some charge. These were charges of profanity, sacrilege, greed, indifference in the form of weariness in the activities of worship, the perversion of moral values, robbery of God, and blasphemy against His holy Name. It is a terrible list and yet in every case the messenger of God complained of these things because of the love of His heart, and so he was endeavoring to show his people through his message, that the deepest sin underlying the sevenfold failure was that they had hurt Him, wounded Him, wronged Him. "I have loved you," in spite of your profanity, sacrilege, greed, indifference, perversion of moral values, robbery, and blasphemy. It was God's word to these failing people. Thus throughout we hear the minor undertone of the wounded heart of God, born of the intensity of His love.

Then we note necessarily that background of failure. In every case at the root of every manifestation of failure there is the fact that the people had failed in their love for God. That failure was not the issue of, but rather the cause. Where there is love for God there will be no profaning of His Temple, no sacrilege, no greed, no refusal to serve, and no weariness in service, no perversion of moral values, no robbery of God, and no blaspheming His Name. With the loss of love for God callousness had resulted as they said, "Wherein hast Thou loved us?" It is true that these people had passed through bitter experiences. The nation had been carried away into captivity, and had endured the horrors of slavery. They had been brought back, but the new city lacked the glory of the former one, and the Temple was so unlike Solomon's in its magnificence that old men wept over it. It may have been that these experiences made them call in question the love of God.

That attitude of mind is not unknown to us. We are sometimes inclined to ask: Why does God allow us to suffer like we are suffering? Why does He lead us through such trying circumstances? Whenever we ask these questions we are tempted to doubt the love of God; and wherever this is so, the deeper fact is that our love for God has grown faint for some reason. We have permitted something to come between us and Himself. We may have kept up the form and ceremonial of religion. We may have attended the Temple, brought the sacrifices into the Church, but we lack love. Love has broken down in us, and caused us to question the love of God for us.

We need to guard our hearts as with a garrison against this questioning of the love of God, which never comes until our own love has somewhere waned and waxed cold. The death of love in us becomes callousness, and there follows a blunted and seared conscience, even while the externalities of religion may be maintained. That is the story of Malachi's days, a story of form without power, of external accuracy and internal heresy.

To that attitude of mind the prophet declared the abiding fact of the love of God. Love is the motive of His government, and their questioning was due to the fact that by some failure in obedience and consequent communion, their own love had ceased to go out towards Him. It is when that is so that we are inclined to question whether God loves us.

Then we come to a radiant revelation of the attitude of God towards the people who constituted a remnant of loyal souls.

As we have said, only a remnant of the people returned from captivity, but within that remnant there was another remnant. The days were chaotic in many respects. There were no kings. They had all passed away. The priesthood was utterly corrupt. Prophecy had been silent for a long period, and was going to be silent again. Nevertheless in the midst of these appalling conditions there were those who were loyal, and their portraiture as given here is very revealing.

"Then they that feared the Lord." We halt with the word "Then." It was when form was rampant, devoid of power, when the people had lost their sense of the love of God, and His love was questioned, when the nation was bringing tithes, but not the whole tithe—a very great difference—when they were saying it was a weariness to wait upon God; then there was a little group of people that are revealed.

Of them we are told:

"They that feared the Lord spake one with another; and the Lord hearkened and heard, and a book of remembrance was written before Him, for them that feared the Lord, and that thought upon His Name. And they shall be Mine, saith the Lord of hosts, in the day that I act."

Two things concerning that group are clearly re-

vealed. The first is that they talked together. "They
. . . spake one with another." In the midst of a de-
generate age there were those who were talking together. In passing, we may say that our Authorized
Version renders it, "They . . . spake often one to
another," but there is no word "often" in the Hebrew.
The statement as Malachi makes it reveals a constant
habit of life, rather than an occasional occurrence.

Then we find what they were talking about as he
tells us that they "thought upon His Name." The conversation would be the result of their thinking. We
tarry a moment with the word "thought." When Paul
wrote, "If there be any virtue and praise," and so forth,
"think on these things," he used the word which is
found in the Septuagint Version of Malachi. Quite
literally it means to take an inventory. These people
thought upon the Name. They were taking an inventory of their wealth in the Name. The kings had gone.
The priests were corrupt. The prophets were silent,
but they still had the Name. To them the Name was
Jehovah. This was variously interpreted at different
times by being connected with other words, such as
Jehovah-Shammah, Jehovah-Tsidkenu, Jehovah-Nissi,
Jehovah-Ropheka. These, and other phrases help to
interpret the wealth of meaning there was in the Name
Jehovah. In that mental activity, resulting in fellowship with others, we find the secret of loyalty in the
midst of decadence.

Then we are told that "the Lord hearkened and
heard." Here once more we pause with words, for Hebrew words are constantly pictorial. In this case the

Lord "hearkened" is an animal word, meaning to prick the ears. The Hebrew word "heard" is also pictorial, and means a bending over, with close attention, so that no sound may be missed. Now our translations would lack final value if we adopted literal translation, but for the moment we are warranted in doing so, and by so doing the statement becomes very arresting. The Lord pricked His ears, and bent down in close attention. Daringly the prophet was attempting to arrest these people by declaring to them that as the horse they might have been driving, would prick his ears to catch the sound of any word that fell from the driver's lips, or as a mother would bend low to miss no syllable of the infant prattle, so God, when these people were talking together, as a result of thinking upon His Name, was listening.

That remnant was the center of real power in the national life, when all else was moribund. The conditions ran on for four hundred years, the great mass of the people formalists, and becoming more and more formal, until they were throttled with their own traditions. But we find in the New Testament, Simeon and Anna, and Joseph and Mary, and others fearing the Lord, talking together as the result of thinking upon His Name. God had said through Malachi, "They shall be Mine in the day that I act,' and they were His vantage ground at the coming of the Messiah.

The last movement in the prophetic message called the people to look on to the coming of another day.

"The day cometh, it burneth as a furnace; and all the proud, and all that work wickedness, shall be stubble; and the day that cometh shall burn them up, saith the Lord of hosts, that it shall leave them neither root nor branch. But unto you that fear My Name shall the sun of righteousness arise with healing in his wings."

The day is to be the same, created by the sun-rising. Its effect will depend upon the conditions of life. The sun rising will burn up stubble, where there is neither root nor life. But it will bring healing where there is life and where there is root. The prophet bade these people look on to that day, and act in accordance with the vision.

The present condition of Christendom is vividly portrayed in Malachi. I did not say, of the Church. I would make a very clear distinction between the Church and Christendom. The Church consists of all those who constitute an elect remnant, that gather together to talk of God, and ever take an inventory of His Name. Christendom is the outward form, and a vast formalism curses it. Let us remember that the day is coming, and when the sun rises, its effect will depend entirely upon our condition of life and character. Stubble it will destroy, but it will bring healing to loyal souls.